MW00986403

How to Cry
on Your Bicycle

How to Cry
ON
YOUR
Bicycle

and other
practical
lessons

Jennaye
Derge

Casa Urraca Press
ABIQUIU

Copyright © 2022 by Jennaye Derge

All rights reserved.

Thank you for supporting authors and artists by buying an authorized edition of this book and respecting all copyright laws by not reproducing, scanning, or distributing any part of it in any form without permission from the author directly or via the publisher, except as permitted by fair use. You are empowering artists to keep creating, and Casa Urraca Press to keep publishing, books for readers like you who actually look at copyright pages.

Set in Calluna and Interstate.
Cover illustration by David Holub.
Author photograph by Kara Cavalca.

25 24 23 22   1 2 3 4 5 6 7

First edition

ISBN 978-1-956375-06-0

CASA URRACA PRESS

an imprint of Casa Urraca, Ltd.
PO Box 1119
Abiquiu, New Mexico 87510
casaurracapress.com

This book is dedicated to my first true love, my baby, and my best friend for more than ten years: my iconic, too-big-for-me, blue 2010 Surly Long Haul Trucker. For a decade this bicycle took me everywhere, anywhere, at any time, and no matter what (unless it had a flat tire or broken chain). It was the best, and I hope whoever owns it now is having as much fun riding it as I did.

Contents

"The most damaging phrase in the language is 'We've always done it this way!'"

Grace Murray Hopper,
computer scientist &
United States Navy rear admiral

Bicycle Baby

I CAUGHT MYSELF CALLING my bicycle "my baby" to someone the other day. As in, I care for my bicycle as much as someone cares for their actual baby. Was this a bit of hyperbole? Yeah, probably. But giving an inanimate object the same credentials as someone's child is okay when you've emptied out your bank account for it and look upon it with pride whenever someone gives it a compliment.

My bicycle is my child because we've been through so much together. It has transported me to first dates and back home from breakups. To job interviews and last days of work. It's taken me home from nights at bars, important business meetings, weddings, and hundreds of job sites. It has transported everything from my groceries and my professional camera equipment to camping necessities and potluck meals.

I've ridden in torrential thunderstorms, hail, winds, ice, and snow. I've pedaled in fancy dresses, costumes, and high heels. Avoided potholes, cars, humans, dogs, deer, and even once a bear cub.

So yeah, my bicycle is my baby because, much like someone's real flesh and blood, my bicycle is also a part of me. Together, we've seen it all, and 1 really don't know what I'd do without it. Perhaps this is dramatic, but if it is ever lost or stolen, I can promise that, when I'm done ugly-crying about it, 1 will put its picture on the side of a milk carton and won't sleep until my baby is safely back in my arms.

Bicycle Commuting

THE DAY I started commuting by bicycle was the day my college professor slammed a chair down on the floor and yelled at the top of his lungs that we're all fucked. And I do believe he used the word *fucked*. It was only a year after the movie *An Inconvenient Truth* came out and the green-wash of modern environmentalism wasn't mainstream yet. The idea had started to take shape in liberal arts colleges like mine and was creeping into the nightmares of students everywhere. And by that, I mean it was being slammed in their faces by passionate sailor-mouthed professors.

It was 2007 and I was an impressionable sophomore in a friendly liberal town who'd come from a pretty sheltered conservative city. I grew up in a place where most everyone around me thought that God, guns, and Hobby Lobby would save us from everything—and if those things didn't, we would just wait for the Second Coming, geared with a Chick-fil-A chicken sandwich in one hand, the bible in the other, and the notorious ex-pastor Ted Haggard cheering us on.

But neither God nor Ted was going to save the planet, and that became abundantly clear to me when my sandals-wearing, curse-word-yelling Intro to Sociology professor told us the world was going to shit. And I do believe he used the word *shit*.

After that class I went home and read our assigned book, *The End of Oil*, which was exactly how it sounds. When I finished, I was terrified and angry about, like, everything. The earth and all living beings on it were being destroyed; people were getting killed, the economy was going to burst, wars were being fought, and it was all for the sake of cheap finite energy, the same kind that ran my car that was sitting in my driveway. So that weekend, I went out and bought a bicycle.

Of course I wasn't actually going to save the world with my clean commute, but riding my bike through those next three years of sociology classes where the subjects were oil depletion, food wars, land theft, and human trafficking made me feel a little better. Under such heavy subjects, I could raise my endorphins on my ride to school. I could pedal my way through every political policy class, and biking gave me something else to focus on rather than the fact that my professor was right. That we are all indeed fucked and the world is most definitely going to shit. But because I couldn't throw chairs and desks, I rode my bike instead.

I rode home after class every day and looked at the view of the mountains from the top of campus. I felt the sun on me when it was sunny and the rain when it was rainy. I flew down the steep hills from campus back into town, clearing my brain and connecting me back to my body.

After I graduated college, I continued to ride my bike everywhere. I had a car but hated to drive it. Bikes were fun; I commuted with fresh air and the sun on me, I always could find a parking spot no matter how full the lots were, and I never had to buy gas.

It's been more than a decade since I read *The End of Oil*, and while I still have people telling me that the world is fucked and we're all going to shit, I don't feel like throwing tables and chairs anymore. I don't ride for the sole purpose of saving the environment or countering the political and social state of the world (although it is a better option than holding up a Bible to the sun or praying to Chick-fil-A) . I ride my bicycle because I can feel the sun on my face, I can see the mountains better, and although I show up sweaty and out of breath everywhere I go, I always show up happy and with a smile.

How to:
Spot a Bicycle Commuter

DEPENDING ON HOW you view bicycle commuters, either they are self-sufficient and eco-conscious folks who independently transport themselves whenever and wherever they want, or they are the asswad friends at the bar who can never be the D.D. because they don't have a car. It's all relative, but no matter what their motives are, they generally all have the same characteristics to easily spot them in the wild.

Bicycle commuters:

- Show up everywhere sweating, out of breath, and with unruly hair.

- Always have bike grease stains on their legs, pants, and sometimes even hands.

- Arrive at every destination in the winter with snot running out of their noses and frozen faces that need a few minutes to defrost.

- Will choose their wardrobe based on whether or not they can bike in it.

- Only refer to a bike seat as a bike *saddle*, which must be expensive and must be leather.

- Will choose romantic partners based on their willingness to also commute by bike.

- Will purchase or carry only objects that fit in a backpack, panniers, or other jury-rigged bicycle contraption.

- Know all the fastest and best ways to get around on backroads, sideroads, or trails, but have trouble giving street directions for cars.

- Hesitate to go anywhere more than five miles away, up really big hills, on cold rainy or snowy days, or after the sun goes down.

- Get mad if there is no bike rack or other place to lock a bike in front of a business.

- Always want to race drivers, betting that their bike can get them anywhere faster.

- Talk about things like bike panniers, braze-ons, shifters, gearing, and various frame metals. This is a favorite pastime.

- Are impatient at stop lights.

- Basically make any and all life decisions based on whether or not they can go by bike.

Thank You
for Sharing
the Road

I'M A RARE BREED in that I'm both an avid road cyclist and also a vehicle driver. So when the repeating argument for who sucks more—road cyclists or vehicles—inevitably goes down, I can easily see both sides.

I've been bike commuting for fifteen years and counting, so I've been on the receiving end of bicycle frustrations. I've been honked at, yelled at, and steamrolled for seemingly no other reason than just being on a bike.

But I've also been driving for seventeen years and counting, and I'd be lying if I said that I've never honked or yelled at a cyclist. Sometimes cyclists are assholes just the same way that vehicle drivers can be. Sometimes I'm all of the above. If you can't spot the asshole, it's probably you.

How to share the road and not be an asshole (for drivers):

- When you park after a long day of work, or a long walk on the beach, or a long whatever, don't just throw open your car door into the street like a rebel throwing caution to the wind. Take a breath, look in your rearview mirrors, and check for bicycles. Car doors usually share the bike lane, and if you open the door when a cyclist is coming, you are, in a way, just punching them with a piece of metal.

- For the love of all things holy, USE YOUR TURN SIGNAL. It's true, we've all forgotten the lost art of non-verbal physical communication, what with emailing, texting, DMing and all, but just think of your turn signal like you're texting bae. "Hey bike bae, psssst. I just wanted to let you know... I'm gonna turn, so proceed with caution." Ooooh yeah—now that's sexty.

- Now bikes sometimes roll through areas where cars are required to stop, and I get it, we live in a land where all rules apply to everyone equally and everything is always fair.

  PSYCH!

  That's not true even in the slightest. When I watch cars roll through stop signs every day, I laugh at the hypocrisy, but that's neither here nor there.

What is both here and there is that nothing is fair, and once you're pushing sixty pounds of metal and groceries between your legs up a big hill and there is a four-way stop with no other cars around, you too will happily thank that great state of Idaho for not only potatoes, but also the Idaho Stop, the bicycle law that allows cyclists to keep going when there's no one else around.

- I love kind and caring strangers. I really do, but when I see cars stop for cyclists where they shouldn't, I want to pull my hair out. What I mean by that is, cars should not stop in the middle of a busy street, when they have the right-of-way, just to allow a bike, who does not have the right-of-way, to cross the street. This causes so much befuddlement for everyone and really what the drivers are doing is putting everyone, including other cars, at danger for crashing into one big pile of metal—including the cyclist. Love you stop thanks bye.

- It's a common understanding that women love being catcalled the same way cyclists love being steamrolled. We cyclists are super impressed by your super big trucks with big fast tires. Tires that kick up dirt and rocks into our faces and hurt our eyes the same way your dirty ugly mug does. If you blind us, how will we give you our phone numbers? We can't, so stop.

- And finally, if you, as a vehicle driver, are blaring some loud music and roll up next to a bicycle commuter on the street, that's cool. Pump that shit up. I'm one hundred percent serious about this one. Roll your window down so the cyclist can hear it better. Moreso if it's Celine Dion or the Avett Brothers—something with heart and soul—because that shit is real and everyone should be able to share that moment with you. Let's be friends and dance it out; let's share this moment together on the road.

How to share the road and not be an asshole (for cyclists):

- Cyclists, you are not invincible! You are not a Lycra-wearing Spider-Man or Jesus or an Instagram or Tik Tok star. You are a human being on a bicycle who CAN be killed by a car. Know that. Chew on it. Read it over and over again like you've read and re-read your Tinder profile. Make sure you've got it down. You can stay alive by following the laws to the best of your abilities. Don't know the laws? I expect that at some point in middle or high school, you learned how to copy people. Copy what cars do. They (generally) watch where they're going, they (try to) yield, they (hopefully) look both ways at stop signs, they (actually not that often) signal, they (usually) don't blast through red lights. Nor do they weave all willy nilly around the road.

Watch for what cars do and mimic them, but from a safe distance so they won't make fun of your Lycra.

All in all, let's just all be respectful, give each other some space, and crank up that Avett Brothers mix. It's a beautiful day in the neighborhood for a ride or a drive. Thank you for sharing the road.

Running Late

I AM NOTORIOUS for running late. And by that, I mean I tend to go on runs that make me late to be somewhere else. Such was the case the other day when I was meeting my friend Luke for happy hour beers just after I'd had an argument with my boyfriend or received a negative email from my boss or something. Whatever the problem was, and with the clock ticking down to happy hour, I laced up my shoes and I went for a short run to clear my head.

I was supposed to just run around the block to release some steam, which I did, but it felt so damn good that I just kept going, just kept releasing steam. I continued my run with the accompaniment of one of my favorite podcasts, *This American Life*, the early years. These Americans' lives (specifically the late

'90s and early 2000s seasons) usually have only small problems—or none at all—and most of the guests on the show overcome all their obstacles by the end of the hour-long radio show—not by running, but by properly dealing, and this is really inspirational to me.

Inspiration, as you may have it, is an energy booster, and the sound of Ira Glass's voice tends to soothe me into a happy running rhythm. So about the time I should have been leaving my house to meet Luke for beer, I was floating across the gravel trail, letting the sun wash over me. I was feeling the breeze touch my skin and letting the squirrels and birds cheer me on as I crested an uphill, and that point made me confident that, if anyone ever needs to deal with life's problems, I'd say run from them.

Like, actually run.

Because even though I was not dealing with any of my problems and actually creating a different problem by being late to meet Luke, I was blissfully unaware of it all and totally engrossed in the trail, in the birds, and in some other American's life instead.

"Wow! That's an incredible story! I can't wait to hear what happened next!" Ira Glass said in my ear. And through my heavy breathing, I thought, *Yeah, me neither!*

By the time I made it back home, showered, and left my house to meet Luke, I was about fifteen minutes late. I sent him a text apologizing and exhaled at his response:

No worries, I'm running late too.

Through my relief, I put my earphones back in for just a minute longer and heard, "We'll be back next week with more stories of this American life." And then I turned the podcast off, said goodbye to my problems, and ran out the door.

How to:
Be Late for
Lunch

11:25 AM — I only have twenty-five more pages in a book I'm reading and I have to finish it.

11:45 AM — My dog just curled up on my lap and he's so cute I don't want to disturb him by getting up.

11:47 AM — I thought I'd try out some lipstick for the hundredth time and it still looks bad and now I have to wash it off.

11:50 AM — I just remembered an email I have to write.

11:52 AM — My shoes are suddenly wrong, which means my pants are wrong, which means my entire outfit is wrong and I have to change.

11:53 AM — My plants look droopy and I have to water all of them so they won't die in the hour that I'm gone.

11:54 AM — I need to download a podcast.

11:56 AM — Someone just called me and, even though I ignored it, I have to wait for them to leave a voicemail and then listen to it.

11:57 AM — My favorite song on Pandora just came on.

11:58 AM — I walked out the door and then realized I had to pee.

12:00 PM — I walked out the door and then realized I forgot to put on deodorant and had to take off my backpack, my coat, and my sweater in order to put it on and then reassemble.

12:02 PM — I walked out the door and then realized I had too many and/or too few layers on and had to completely change my outfit again.

12:05 PM — I forgot where we were going for lunch, so I had to look it up.

12:08 PM — I realized it was within walking distance, so I decided to walk.

12:12 PM — I ran into someone I haven't seen in a long time and had to catch up.

12:20 PM — I ran into someone I see all the time, but we still had to catch up.

12:32 PM — I couldn't find where you were sitting.

12:45 PM — You left because I was so late to lunch.

New Bike Day

I RECENTLY BOUGHT a brand new mountain bike in a fashion that is totally *me*: spontaneously, semi-irresponsibly, and in a hurry because I was late to be somewhere.

I had been half-heartedly looking to buy a new bike for years, looking in local bike shops, drooling at the shiny frames, and glaring at friends' bikes the same way I look at uneaten pieces of pizza: "Hey, you gonna ride that? If not, can I have it?"

I could never pull the trigger, though, until a few weeks ago when I went to a local bike shop to "browse."

Within mere moments, a very nice salesman found me. "May I help you?" he asked. His smile was vibrant. I swear the heavens opened up and the angels sang his praises.

"Well... actually..." I said, eyeing a nearby bike.

He looked me in the eyes with a non-verbal *I understand exactly why you're here, and you can trust me* look. He gave me a nod, and asked me to follow him upstairs where all the brand-new mountain bikes lived.

My heart beat harder and then subsequently dropped when I saw the price tags, but my charming salesman took the cue. "What if we give you a little... deal?" he said.

He went over and sat at a computer, typing things in and taking numbers off. I stood there nervously biting my lip. I was NOT planning on buying a mountain bike that day, but he was making it hard to say no.

As if on cue, my friend called me, wondering where I was. I was supposed to be meeting him for lunch precisely ten minutes before. I thanked the salesman and raced down the stairs and out the door, but instead of going to lunch, I went to the bank to figure out if I had enough money to impulsively buy a brand new mountain bike.

"No no no." My level-headed friend stopped me in my mania. "There's another place with cheaper bicycles. Let's go there."

We arrived to a fleet of bicycles lined up outside the shop, and although I was just spotting them from afar, I knew I had found "the one."

"The one" would have to wait, though. Checking the time, I realized I was late to a meditation class.

Yes... meditation. Amongst all this purchasing anxiety and bike searching, I needed to go sit in a zen state for ninety minutes. How that was going to happen at that particular time in my particular state of bicycle-buying anxiety I had no idea, but I knew that I couldn't leave this bike behind.

"You can take it home overnight," the bike shop owner said.

Was he proposing a one night stand? This guy was clever. Of course I'd become attached after a night with the bike. The moment I said okay was the moment I basically sealed the deal for our relationship. If this bike was coming home with me that night, it was coming home with me forever, and in my meditation class, my monkey brain led me to believe this was true.

Ommmm. I was sitting in the back of the class, breathing... in... out... *ommmmmygod am I really going to buy a bike?...* in... *should I spend that much money?...* out... *I can't wait to try my new dropper post!*

The next morning I rode back to the bike shop, and when the owner asked me if I wanted to commit, I said "I do," gave him just enough money to leave me with food and housing, and walked out with my two-wheeled, full-suspension, 29er soulmate and a friend who I was late to meet for lunch.

Strava

THERE'S SUCH A THING as healthy competition, and then there's Strava.

Strava, the popular athlete's training app, isn't unhealthy per se, but anxiety is, and every once in a while I blame Strava for my mid-recreation stress. Strava is great, or whatever, because it tracks every tiny movement a person makes when they run, bike, or swim on an app that is obviously meant for triathletes and not for people who just want to take their dog on a routine morning jaunt.

If you use it, you'll notice that it follows you by GPS and records all your stats including pace, elevation, and your hopes and dreams. Then it saves all this data into geographical segments so that next time you do even slightly worse on that big uphill, it can shame you into crying before you even start your Monday.

If you actually do better than one of your previous stats, though, it gives you a little medal, and that feels good and ultimately makes you want to do better to get more medals.

So, you can see why it's so popular; it uses shame and rewards and all the other things we're psychologically addicted to, and that's probably why I downloaded it on my phone to begin with. That, and so I could be in "healthy competition" with myself. I wanted to see my stats, get the little medals, and try to make it up that big hill without crying. I wanted to be faster, stronger, and better—that is, until I suddenly started getting followers.

I had the app for a few weeks before I realized it was a social app; my friends could also see the days where I couldn't make it up the hill, and they quite possibly saw me cry, too. They could see the days where I didn't earn any medals or the days—or, weeks—I didn't go out at all. While I personally may have come to peace with popcorn and Netflix instead of "crushing" and "sending," I can't be certain that my Strava friends could. All this "following" made me feel a little self-conscious, anxious, and therefore, slightly unhealthy.

The thing is, I always had a legitimate excuse as to why my Strava stats were lower today than yesterday, but neither the app nor my friends could possibly know that on Monday I had a toe cramp and so I crawled at snail-speed and on Tuesday I had too much coffee so I went fast and far. Wednesday I had a ton of work to do and a huge deadline so I went for an impromptu long run and Thursday was a thousand degrees outside so I just melted my way back home.

My obvious next step with Strava was to change my settings to "private" and ignore all my follower requests, but I still became anxious on days with a headwind or when I brought my dog along and he needed to stop and sniff something. Slowing down for any reason meant my stats would be compromised and I wouldn't get my medals and I needed my medals—give me my medals!

This "healthy competition" was truly bringing out the worst in me even when I was just competing with myself. So one day while running, I decided to create my own version of a running and biking app that gives or takes away points based on situational variables, awarding you points when there is an unavoidable hindrance and taking away points if you have any noteworthy advantages. Making things a little more fair, a little less stressful, and a little more healthy.

How to Strava in a way that makes everything fair and therefore is actually healthy:

- It's a beautiful day. The weather is perfect; not too hot, not too cold. You're feeling great, perfect for a run: **0 POINTS**

- You got in a fight with your significant other and that makes your blood pulse and your endorphins soar so you run harder: **-3 POINTS**

- A storm front is moving in and you have a headwind of thirty MPH: **+3 POINTS**

- You turned around so the storm front is giving you a tailwind of forty-five MPH: **-5 POINTS**

- Now it's raining, snowing, and hailing all at the same time: **+4 POINTS**

- Maybe just give up on running and go get a bicycle instead. Don't forget to use Strava on your rides.

How to:
Use Trails

I TRY MY DARNDEST to get out on some sort of trail every day. Ideally, and to impress everyone by saying this, I run on a trail every morning. If I don't run, I get on a mountain bike. If I don't ride, I take my dog for a walk. If I can't even do that, I leave a trail of popcorn from the kitchen to my bedroom, and since I'm walking on it, it's a real trail.

The rules on each of those trails are textbook: right-of-way, leave no trace, smile at passerby, and leash and pick up after your dog. But these rules have been thrown out the window and replaced by total. and. complete. anarchy.

There is at least one of these lawless trails in every town; they connect places geographically but tear everyone apart emotionally. It is damn near every man, dog, and child for himself: users leaving traces, practicing wrong-of-way, and yelling at passerby, with dogs running freer than motel shampoo samples.

When I'm out on the trails, on my morning run, or rolling through on my morning commute, these "freedom dogs" zig and zag in front of me. One time a dog ran in front of my bike and caused me to crash. But dog laws are as old as dirt and we've all been dealing with them and breaking them since the dog-gone dawn of time, and I'm not here to change any-one's minds or their dogs. What I am here to do, though, is change rules.

Gather up, y'all. There are some new laws in town.

Trail Rule #1:

Always smile at passersby and engage in friendly conversation shall it arise. Trails are meant for every-one, and we should all be kind and friendly to each other. Unless you're passing someone who is running to the point of total exhaustion; leave them alone. Don't ask questions, don't make pleasantries, don't even smile, because while you might want to make a friend, that person is really just trying not to die.

Trail Rule #2:

Uphill questions are mean. Asking friends questions while they're trying to catch their breath going uphill on a trail is just bad etiquette. Hold trail questions, pleasantries, flirtations, meaningful conversations, jokes, etc. for easier parts of the trail. Though you may do this to frenemies and friends you're mad at, because it makes them suffer.

Trail Rule #3:

If you're a hiker and/or you describe your general speed as "sauntering," that's totally fine. I, too, am a bit of a rambler. But please know that "on your left" means that someone is trying to pass you on your left. I know it can be confusing because maybe you think the person is telling you to go left, or maybe you were just surprised or caught off guard. I get it. I'm also a nervous walker. But—and now this is important—even if you do end up going left instead of right, that's actually totally fine, but please stay there. Just pick a side, whatever side, doesn't matter, and stay there. What you shouldn't do is jump left, and then right, and then left again, and then stop and look at the L's on your hands to figure out which way is left before jumping left again.

Walking on a trail isn't hopscotch and we're not on hot lava.

Trail Rule #4:

Similarly, if you're in a group, please move in unison. If you all scatter like frightened deer in every direction,

I can't confidently say that I won't run you through with my bike.

Trail Rule #5:

If you are coming up behind people on your bicycle super fast yelling "on your left" because you're late to feed your cats, that's fine. Ride like the wind, dear one. Yeehaaww. Do be aware, though, and respectful of the saunterers. Ring your bells, honk your horns, and give folks ample time to play hopscotch on lava until they land in a spot with room for you to pass. Your unfed cat will survive if you have to take a second to pause, I promise.

Yes, it's a lawless world out there. The proverbial guns are drawn, saloon doors are swinging, trash is blowing in the wind, the scent of dog poop is in the air. The moment anyone steps on that dusty trail, democracy is out. Someone has to make the rules. So saddle up, ladies and gents. There's a new sheriff on these trails, and she wants you to be aware, be kind, and leash up your dog.

You Can Skip
the Hellos

Trail etiquette has always been important to me. Not, like, eat-your-daily-fruits-and-veggies-and-walk-the-dog important, but enough to where I notice when someone is being a dick on the trail.

I feel the need to say hello to everyone I pass on any trail, no matter what I'm doing, and this has, on more than one occasion, caused an issue and maybe even made me lose a few friends.

I know, right? The opposite of what you'd expect.

The thing is, when you're leisurely walking in the woods, it's absolutely fine to say hello to whomever you pass. There's no reason not to stop and ask a passing familiar face how things are and catch up on each other's lives. Seeing a friend on the trail is a delight when you're going slow and are breathing at a relatively normal rate. When you're dressed in your hiking clothes and look, for the most part, the same as you do in everyday life.

When you are running or biking, however, I'd maybe just skip it.

Skip the hellos and pleasantries when you're passing by someone who is breathing hard. Even if it's your friend you haven't seen in a couple months—just skip it. Trust me with this one, as just the other day I tried to say hello to my friend on the trail and it was a complete and utter disaster. All the pieces were perfectly in place to have what normally should be a pleasant experience, and yet it turned into a pathetically embarrassing moment for the both of us—scarring our egos for as long as we choose.

The ingredients were all there: she was running, I was mountain biking. I had all my bike gear on, which renders me mostly unrecognizable to most people who haven't already seen me in it; the only reason I recognized her red, sweaty face was because her dog was there, and I know her dog. We were passing by each other, each heaving and hoing through burning lungs, and at the very last second, when we knocked elbows in passing, I stupidly decided to yell out her name.

"Sarah!"

Sarah knew she was Sarah, but she did not know I was me, so not only did we both lose our forward momentum, but we also lost our focus. She had to stop to try to figure out who I was under the helmet and sunglasses, and I had to stop to just stare because I didn't recognize that she didn't recognize. So, we both just stood there on the trail, staring at each other, not knowing what to do or say, until finally she yelled out my name in only semi-confident recognition. She apologized profusely, I apologized back, and then we laughed and went our separate ways—her learning what I look like under my bike helmet, and me learning that some etiquette rules are made to be broken.

RBF

I WOULDN'T SAY I have a resting bitch face, but other people would. My lips tend to point downward on their edges, and I catch myself furrowing my brows when I do almost anything. I like to blame it all on my family heritage, but other than that, it's just who I am.

Some people comment on my natural frown in sly ways by asking questions like, "What's wrong?" when nothing's wrong. Or, "Is everything okay?" when everything is totally okay. This really started to get to me over the years. *Why does everyone always think I'm not okay?*

AM I okay?

Really what it is, though, is that I just don't walk around with a beaming smirk on my face all day.

I don't walk down the sidewalk with a cheery smile, or any smile really, and despite my biologically German grimace, I'm actually naturally quite happy and I really do love smiling and being friendly. Unfortunately, though, I physically default to a concerned bitch when I go about my day, running errands, riding my bike, and other normal things.

I have been told that I don't look normal. I look pissed. For that, I would like to give a blanket apology to all those folks who have passed by me over the years and thought that I was not okay. I want to take this moment to say sorry to those who have wanted to acknowledge me in a friendly manner when I, unknowingly, just frowned in return.

I'm sorry that my genetics may have made my aura a little assholey, but I assure you, I do not mean to be. When you smile or say hi at me while we pass on the street or the trail, I am probably okay, nothing's wrong. I'm sorry, it's just my face, resting.

Grocery Stores

I DON'T LIKE to use the phrase "there are two types of people in this world" because there are many types of humans that I love and embrace, and I'll always support everyone's choices in life. Except when it comes to the grocery store, and then there are two types of people in this world: amazing people who hate the grocery store, and people who love the grocery store.

I fall in the former category; I hate the grocery store and I don't really understand people who like it. I crinkle my eyebrows, cock my head, and sputter out *but... why?* when anyone has anything positive to say about the place where fruits and vegetables go to die.

Yes, It's hard for me to understand anyone getting excited to walk through a fluorescent-lit maze of screaming children, turtle-slow men, and angry business ladies who also happen to be standing in front of the toothpaste I want.

It's also difficult to find pleasure in conscientiously perusing sale items when a wake of vulture shoppers suddenly crowds around me and reaches for the same marinara sauce I want. And never have I ever, ever turned to any of those marinara-stealing, mouth-breathing vultures and thought, *Wow, I really love it here!*

But, I've slowly learned that there are those people in the world who really do love it there.

And you can easily spot them because they will be walking slowly up and down every single aisle as if they are explorers in the rainforest on an epic search for the elusive unicorn monkey. They *ooh* and *ahh* at the yellow two-for-five-dollar sales tags, and they stare at ingredients on cereal boxes like they're Sherlock fucking Holmes and that box of Cocoa Puffs is a clue. They have Food Network recipes glowing on their phones and a Starbucks cup sitting in their carts. You can spot grocery store lovers because they stand in the frozen food aisle feeling, not cold, but *happiness*.

They feel happy when the self-scanner blares the cost of the toilet paper at its highest volume. They don't seem to mind the impatient guy behind them in line whistling a blank, non-melodious tune. They don't even seem to notice the random bump-ins with ex-lovers and their new girlfriends and the awkward small talk that goes with them. Not only don't they mind these things, they are blissfully unaware of them, which is perhaps why loving the grocery store is so easy.

Sometimes I wish I was one of these people; I really do. I wish I wanted to go to the grocery store before my cupboards went bare. I wish I didn't force myself to make a charcuterie of leftover food for dinner just so I can avoid the store one more day.

Instead, I will go grocery shopping when it's dire. And when I finally do, I know exactly what I need and where those things are. I will avoid certain busy times of the day and eye contact with people I know so as to not get stuck in a conversation that will prolong my time under the fluorescent lights.

And while I unhappily walk through the the aisles of food I don't need, I will continue thinking about the two kinds of people in the world; the ones who love the grocery store, and the people like me who are normal and will run away from the sliding glass doors as fast as they can.

The Domestic Skeptic

I DON'T COOK. Or rather, I choose not to cook. If given the right ingredients and tools, I can, and have, but for the most part I just don't.

It's a hard thing to admit and gets the same reaction as someone saying they don't like Betty White or revealing that Santa is really Dad. The truth is shocking and it hurts, but so does holding a hot, heavy sauté pan.

I could blame my allergy to cooking on my small studio's oven-less kitchenette or my mini-fridge that has just enough room for some moldy leftovers, but my distaste for the culinary started long before my lack of kitchen space. I believe my cook-phobia stems from my innate hatred for clutter—keeping me away from things like spice racks and pantry foods—and also from my frugality that runs deep in my bloodline. If I have the extra cash floating around, I probably won't be spending it on Le Creuset, blenders, or things like "ingredients" and "cutlery." I will probably spend it on a fourth and fifth bicycle that I most definitely need more.

I understand that my aversion to pulling pies out of the oven doesn't bode well for male suitors, and I've probably been left out of a few potluck invite lists because of it, but that's perfectly fine with me. I do not want to ooze with domesticity. To my knowledge, none of my childhood diaries ever read "I want to grow up to be just like Julia Child!"

Who I am is more of a snacker. Or a put-together-whatever-I-have-in-the-fridge-er. I'm a creature of habit, and I generally buy the same things at the grocery store week after week. I know the foods that I enjoy and when the sudden hunger hits—which it always does in a pinch—I don't have to scratch my chin and say *hmmm, what should I have for dinner?* I already know what I'm going to have for dinner: pretty much what I had for dinner last night.

I might make it with a little flair and yes, if the music hits me right, I might even turn it into a meal. I might do a little sautéing or mixing and throw in what few spices I do have room for on my small shelf, but usually snacking through dinnertime suffices for me.

I understand that this way of eating sounds terribly boring and that I may lead a mundane existence because of it, but trust me when I say that my non-cooking in no way reflects my everyday life, which is full of flavor and spice if I do say so myself. Nor does it mean I hate food—on the contrary, I actually love food. Like, LOVE it. On the right day with the right people I will totally go out of my way for a good meal. I love complex colors and flavors on my plate; a nice glass of wine, maybe a sip of whiskey or scotch and some Billie Holiday or Bing Crosby playing in the background; *yeah, that's smooth.* Or some tacos from a taqueria, a built up fancy burger, sweet potato fries. Yeah, yum, I love that stuff. But that stuff does not happen every day, and thank goodness for that. So in the meantime, my kitchen-grazing without an apron, oven, or spice rack will have to do just fine.

Tupperware

LEFTOVERS ARE a glorified entity in my life. When I cook, I do it knowing that I hate it, so I do it in bulk. The more leftovers I have to hold me over, the longer it will be until I have to cook again.

Such was the case the other night when I cooked significantly too much rice for one meal. When I went into my cabinets to find a container to store my excess rice, I found dozens of pieces of Tupperware and not one lid to fit any of them.

Instead of getting angry, though, I wrapped the lidless Tupperware with the kind of Saran wrap that doesn't stick to anything but itself. Then I took a pen that didn't actually exist because, you know, pens are also never available when you need them, and I "wrote" *Tupperware* on my proverbial grocery store list before going to the store to buy Tupperware—and pens. When I got to the food storage aisle, I stood in front of the six different shelves of Rubbermaid, Glad, Martha Stewart, etc. There was plastic Tupperware and glass Tupperware, there were round ones, square ones, and ones shaped like a single slice of pizza. There were cups and jugs, and sets of five, ten, twenty, pink, blue, yellow, BPA free, microwave safe, and (apparently) microwave unsafe. Ones with little compartments and ones so big I could fit a full meal in them. I tried to imagine my leftovers in any and all versions. *Would my leftovers look good in that one? Would my leftovers be happy?*

The prices ranged from five dollars to fifty and some had discount sales tags on them but came with a choking hazard warning, or a picture of a creepy cartoon character. I kneeled down to read the containers' details so many times that I kept getting dizzy and my quads burned. When people would walk in front of me to get by, I became annoyed, and when they stopped to also look at the Tupperware, even more so. When the bakery called for the deli department to answer line two on the speaker, I lost my breath and had to lean on a shelf. I was stuck in the grocery store, getting hungry and all the more confused with each and every Tupperware option—the situation was getting dire and it was getting difficult for me to maintain my composure, so I finally made a decision.

I bet I can find Tupperware at a thrift store for a fraction of the cost.

I breathed a sigh of relief at this revelation and was proud of my critical thinking and my ability to save money because of it. I left the grocery store empty-handed, save for a bag of rice which I cooked too much of that night and then Saran-wrapped up in a Tupperware container that had no lid.

How to:
Marie Kondo

I WAS SLOW on hearing about this Marie Kondo person. Her name became popular about a year before I even learned about her tidying-up concept, but as soon as I did I was immediately bothered. She's truly going out on a limb by telling me that the only things between me and true happiness are the pile of rarely worn clothes sitting in my closet and the box of yarn I'll never use.

But Marie Kondo has been telling people to get rid of their old junk in order to "spark joy" for a long time now, and she has somehow squeezed her way into our homes to make us believe that what we were already calling "spring cleaning" is a life-changing psychological phenomenon—and for that, I suppose, she is our hero.

Whether you want to call it "sparking joy," "spring cleaning," or "just checking off boxes on the honey-do list," it is never too late to start dusting off the cobwebs, clearing out your closet, and asking that old desk lamp if it brings you joy. And since Marie K is busy changing the world with closet organizers, I'm here to help.

How to Marie Kondo, my way:

- First, walk into your chosen room that needs organizing. Close your eyes, breathe in deep, open your eyes, and take a look around. Panic. Allow your heart to race from the sheer overwhelm of clutter. Stop. Turn around and leave your house immediately. Go to your local liquor store and get a bottle of your choice. Make a cocktail and start drinking.

- Next, go back to the room, take another deep breath, take another sip of your cocktail, and pick up an object. Stare at it for longer than you should ever stare at an object and ask yourself if it brings you joy (preferably silently, but out loud if you're really serious). If the object barks or meows, set it down. It is your pet, and even though Spot ate your gloves yesterday, he does bring you joy and you should keep him.

- Then, sort your objects into piles of "yes, this brings me joy" and "no, this does not bring me joy" and stare at the two piles for a while whilst changing your mind and shuffling objects between piles a dozen times. Give up, take a cocktail break.

- Next, wobble back into your room and be that go-getter you've always wanted to be. You CAN make decisions! You aren't tied to things! You got this! We believe in you! Package up your items to take to the thrift store and then go to bed—it's been a big day. Good work, sport. Let's try again tomorrow.

- When you wake up in the morning and realize you have a hangover, throw all alcohol in the trash. It does not bring you joy anymore. Then go back to your project room and collect all the packaged-up objects that don't bring you any joy. Remember that you don't hate these objects, they just don't make you outwardly happy, so refrain from throwing them out the window with rage and yelling at no one for no particular reason.

- Finally, donate your objects. Before leaving the thrift store, close your eyes, breathe in deep, open your eyes in gratitude. Take a look around. Start shopping. Spend the next hour or so running around trying on clothes and looking at objects. They all bring you joy, so purchase everything, including Marie Kondo's new bestselling book, then go home and do it all again.

Good job. Marie Kondo would be proud.

New Year's Resolutions

I WAS TALKING to a friend the other night about New Year's resolutions and he told me that last January first he resolved to start flossing. Flossing seems easy and practical enough, except that he never did it. He didn't even floss on the first day of the New Year or the second or the third. He went months without flossing and thus never resolved his new year. So, in honor of his noncommittal resolutions, here are a few that I'd be pretty happy doing, but also totally fine if I didn't:

- Answer the phone—not just let it go to voicemail—when someone calls.

- Use actual bookmarks instead of random things like Kleenex, ChapStick, or tea bag wrappers.

- Wear socks without holes in them.

- Finish a full bottle of salad dressing before buying a new one.

- Finally go ad-free on Pandora.

- Stop telling people my bike is my baby.

- Start stocking up on things like toilet paper, shampoo, and food so they don't run out when I need them.

- Maybe use the thumbs-up emoji in text messages less often.

- Clean out my email inbox.

- Water my plants before they look droopy.

- stop calling a carton of strawberries a "meal."

- Start flossing.

I think it's going to be a pretty good year.

Mercury Retrograde

I CAN'T REMEMBER when I first heard about the ill-omened astrological phenomenon "Mercury retrograde," but when I did, I'm sure I reacted like a lot of people—i.e., *That's a bunch of hooey poppycock wizardry! Planets can't move backward, let alone discombobulate my life so hellishly!* And then I probably dropped my cell phone in the toilet and sat in melted chocolate.

Mercury retrograde, in its simplest scientific form, is when the planet Mercury appears to be moving backward. Mind you, it doesn't actually move backward, it's just a rotational illusion seen from earth by sky scientists. In its poppycock wizardry form—the one I'm most concerned with—it is when our lives just totally and completely fall apart. This retrograde period lasts for three weeks and happens three to four times a year, and during the retrograde, everything sucks. Electronics and communication go haywire, everyone is late to everything, deals and contracts fall through, someone from your past sneaks up, tensions run high, and the only safe thing is to hide in a dark corner and do nothing and talk to no one.

One such tri-annual doom-period began recently on a day that I was talking to my neighbors about their parents' airplane flight that kept getting delayed. I can't remember who said it first, but we all muttered the words "Mercury" and "retrograde" at a relatively similar time. We collectively laughed and then denied that we truly believed in it, but then my neighbors left to go pick up their parents whose luggage got lost and they arrived back home almost three hours late. And that, my friend—that—is Mercury retrograde.

For the next three weeks, between the five of my neighbors, we experienced a destroyed electronic, a bicycle that was ripped off the top of the car by a too-low drive-thru, the loss of a job, and a lost cat. We mumbled and texted each other these events with our personal damnations against Mercury, and I brushed it off for the most part until I had to travel. It was a one-week trip to Missoula, Montana, for my friend's wedding, and while I kept my chin high, I could feel the storm clouds roll in, and that they did. On the day of the wedding, a hail storm clobbered the couple and the ceremony. The day after, a tree fell over in the middle of the matrimonial property. On my way back home to Colorado, I almost missed my flight because the airport's electronic check-in system was down, and then I literally bumped into an estranged friend and her husband while dashing to my gate.

You can call it phony, you can call it a scapegoat for bad luck, it doesn't matter to me. All that matters is the minute the retrograde is over. I count down the days to when there will be no more reasons for me to run into any of my exes (I ran into two of them during the retrograde), to say something stupid to anyone (just kidding, that's always on the table), or to be overly sensitive about safeguarding my electronics.

Once a retrograde is over, we can all start making plans, signing contracts, and traveling again, but if you miss your airplane flight because you dropped your phone in your ex's toilet—well, you can't blame it on Mercury once it's no longer in retrograde. You just have terrible luck.

Three
Great Loves

MOST TWENTY-ONE-YEAR-OLDS receive free drinks and shots with cute names like "birthday cake" and "muff diver" for their birthdays. On my twenty-first birthday, I received my life's prophecy.

I nannied for a friend's young son, and whenever I wasn't changing diapers or playing with trains, she and I hung around talking about the amazing unknowns of the world. "The universe works in mysterious ways," she'd say.

She owned books written by a man who believed our futures, our love matches, and our personality characteristics could be determined by the date of our birth, and when I borrowed the books, I read them even deeper.

Then about a month before my birthday, she arranged a phone call for me with the prophecy man. To this day, it haunts me. Almost everything he told me was spot on: who I am as a person, what my past was like, and what my future would resemble.

But the thing that really stuck with me—haunted me then and still to this day—was his prophecy for my "three great loves."

He told me I would have three great loves before I met the person I'd happily spend the rest of my life with.

While I was on that phone call, I was already dating someone I liked very much. In fact, I believed at that time that I loved him. I was moving into a small cabin on a lake with him before we took off to backpack around South America for three months. If that isn't some sort of love, I don't know what is. But after I got off the phone call with the fortune man, I saw my boyfriend differently. When I looked him in the eyes, I thought in the back of my head that sooner or later we would break up. That I still had three loves before I met the person I'd end up with. No matter if he was one of the three or not, I was told, it would end.

To this day I wonder if I subconsciously sabotaged the relationship because of this fortune telling. I don't think I did; I think the relationship just ended when it was supposed to end, but it's still hard not to wonder.

My next great love was not ready for love, but that didn't stop him. His fiancée had just broken up with him after a long, tumultuous relationship. He also happened to be my friend and, moreso, friends with my recent ex. But he went through all the hoops to get to me: he asked my ex for his blessing, he always came to see me at my job, and then he lured me in with a hot tub on a hill, under a glowing moon and romantic night sky. All the pieces were there, and it clicked into place.

He was a good one, and we had one heck of a time. We went rock climbing any spare second we had, and he introduced me to mountain biking—sometimes we did both in one day. He was kind, friendly, and always excited and ready for a good time, but he wasn't ready for the love to get any greater, and somewhere deep inside me, I knew it all along.

Just a few months after that breakup, I met my next great love. He'd had his eye on me even before I ended things with my previous boyfriend. He was tall, handsome, and apparently everywhere. Unbeknownst to me, we ran into each other frequently, but I never remembered because his face just couldn't stick in my brain. He was also just out of a long relationship—a marriage in fact—and also would come to visit me at my job. Then, one day, his face finally stuck. He sent me a sweet email asking me out, and after I said yes, we had our own long, tumultuous relationship.

And there they were, the three great loves. I'm coming up on my thirty-third birthday now, just over a decade after the birthday when the fortune man predicted these relationships. Were these it? Were these the "three great loves"? What even is a "great love"? I told all three of these men that I loved them, but I can't say with certainty that I loved any of them greatly. Thinking back on the prophetic phone call, I remember the man said these relationships would change me, and there's no doubt in my mind that they did, but now what? I haven't spoken to the woman who set me up with the fortune reader for years now. Life took us separate ways, but I still think back to her reassurances that the universe does indeed work in mysterious ways.

Please Perfectly Fill in the Bubbles

TODAY I VOTED. It took longer for me to fill out my ballot than I'd expected, longer than I'd like to admit to any of my friends or family, but nonetheless, I received my "I voted" sticker and I've never felt more relieved.

I felt more relief than excitement because, although I've always believed in democracy, I spent weeks avoiding my mail-in ballot as it got covered by junk mail, magazines, and whatever else I threw on my Bermuda Triangle coffee table. But just knowing it was there, untouched, flamed my guilt and became a beacon of my procrastination.

Okay, yes, it's me! I shouted in my head every time I passed the coffee table and saw my name in print on the unopened envelope. *It's me who hasn't voted!* And once I started outwardly seething with this guilt, the whole world seemed to shout at me.

First, the canvassers came.

"Just checking to make sure you've filled out and returned your ballot!" The canvassers were usually really nice and charming and had beautiful smiles. Most of them were, strangely, attractive males about my age. I wondered if their agencies were trying a new tactic this year.

"Uhh, duh! Like of course I have, like, totally, already turned it in! Omg." I'd giggle and twirl my hair to charm and distract the man-vassers from seeing my unopened ballot screaming from the coffee table behind me. "SHE'S LYING! HERE I AM, UNOPENED!"

The internet was worse.

"Good morning!" my email account said. "Have you voted yet?"

Google yelled at me to vote in various languages many times over. "HAVE YOU VOTED YET????"

The full content of the internet was shrieking at me.

"FILL ME OUT!" my ballot screamed from the coffee table.

"REMEMBER TO VOTE!" I swore I heard the man-vasser say outside my door.

I rubbed my throbbing head and closed my laptop.

I paced my house and then opened my laptop again.

I had work to do.

I needed to do some research. It was pretty obvious who I'd choose for president, but I still needed to know about amendments, propositions, senators, and judges.

I formed my opinions, chose my sides, and grabbed a blue or black pen.

The moment had come, and there I sat at the Bermuda Triangle coffee table, hands sweating and shaky, ready to make my voice heard, ready to make sure this terrible man didn't become our president. I read the instructions carefully, like I do any official form, and paused at "Please perfectly fill out these bubbles."

"What does 'perfectly' *mean*?" My hands shook even more. "What if I accidentally make a wrong mark? There is a lot riding on this election. Will *he* become president because of *my* mistake?"

My nerves were getting the best of me.

"All you have to do is fill me out," my ballot tried to assure me. "*JUST FILL ME OUT!*"

When I finally finished and signed and dated the envelope, I placed the pen down carefully, wiped off my sweat, and sighed in relief. I did it. I perfectly filled in the bubbles.

A Date with Don

(The following events are loosely based on three real-life dates but mixed with a good dose of poetic license.)

IN NOVEMBER 2016, my boyfriend and I broke up. I fell into a deep funk, and my worried friends, understandably, did what any good friends do: they got me drunk and signed me up for an online dating app.

They swiped for me in the comfort of our whiskey blankets, and then, when I got home, I forgot about anyone I matched with except one.

His name was Don and his profile caught my eye.

"Hey Don, you sound really interesting!" I sent. "If you'd ever want to hang out, message me!"

It was three A.M. when I got my first red flag.

"Hey grabbable woman, I also love covfefe. I'd love to get dinner sometime and tell you how I've become such a really, really, great and important person. I'm really incredible. You should see my tie collection."

This should have stopped me in my tracks, but his dating profile was so intriguing that I went along with it.

So we set up a time to meet at a local brewery. When I arrived, I looked around until I spotted a single gentleman sitting at the bar talking on his phone and fixing his hair in the reflection of the window. I tried to figure out if it was indeed the man from the app, for he looked nothing like his profile picture.

As I got closer, he looked at me, pointed at his phone, and mouthed, *Just a minute.* I waved an understanding hand and mouthed back, *No problem.*

"Babe, babe, babe, don't worry babe, it'll all be okay," he said into the phone.

He paused, and I wondered who "babe" was.

"Oh, baby, don't worry! You're one in a million," he cooed.

He finally said bye to his mistress and turned toward me. "Sorry, that was just my daughter, she's having some business problems, but I rate her as a million," Don explained. "You know, you remind me a lot of my daughter, and my ex-wife." He sized me up.

He, on the other hand, looked nothing like anyone I knew or anything I'd ever seen. He was obviously not the handsome gentleman I had swiped. But maybe he had a great personality. After all, I reasoned, with enough beer anyone can have a great personality.

"Can I get you guys some beer?" the bartender asked right in the nick of time.

"She'll have a burger and a beer," Don said to the bartender. "And I'll have a salad and water."

He sniffled and turned away from the bartender, brushing him off to retrieve our beverages.

"So tell me about yourself," Don said to me. Then without letting me respond and all in one breath, he said, "I have a bigly house. You must rent. You look like you rent."

"Yeah, I rent. It's so expensive to buy here," I replied.

"You got renters insurance? You need to have renters insurance. Renters insurance is a very big deal. A very, very bigly deal. All of the great, wonderful people have renters insurance," he said, waving his fist.

"No," I sheepishly replied.

The bartender placed my beer in front of me, and I guzzled.

"I know a lot of people, a lot of really great people, and I have a lot of money and all those really great people I know, they really love me, they really very much love me, and they all have renters insurance!" Don said.

"Okay, I'll look into it," I stammered before changing the subject. I tried referring to his online dating profile, which was quickly becoming apparent he had fabricated. "So, you said you like mountain biking?"

"Oh yes, biking. Biking is great and I'm the best mountain biker ever. You should see my very expensive bicycle. It is one of a kind and very very good. It is the best bicycle. Very expensive. Made by the best company. I own the best company. None of the other companies are as great as my company. My company makes a lot of people happy, very, very happy. Without my company people couldn't live. Or own things like shoes. Shoes are the greatest, my shoes are the greatest shoes—they are white shoes, white shoes are the only shoes anyone should wear. White shoes are the best shoes, they are very, very good," he said, salad coming out of his mouth.

"Neat..." I said. "So, Don, that's a weird name. Where is it from?"

"AMERICA!" he yelled, and then continued: "Don is what is known in America as a nickname. Nicknames are what make American names great again!"

"Okay... cool," I mustered.

Don looked at me confused, like I should be more excited by all the greatness. He pursed his lips, squinted at me, and without breaking eye contact snapped his fingers at the bartender for the check and then got up to leave.

"Well, this was really, really, really, great. I'm really great. I'm the greatest, millions of people gather in my presence, and my hands are yuge," he said as he put on his jacket and checked out his reflection again. "I'll send you a text message if I ever have the time to see you again. I have the best text messages. Many people call them Tweets but my text messages are received and read by five hundred billion million people."

"Okay, bye," I said, confused but also a little relieved.

As he walked out the door, he turned around, the wind folding his hair over in the wrong direction, his spray tan glowing in the fluorescent light. He squinted into my eyes, and with pursed lips and furrowed brow, he said, "You should really get renters insurance."

And then he walked out of my life forever.

The Power
to Choose

I WAS A FRESHMAN in college when my mom found out I had popped my cherry. I wasn't planning to tell her, not because I didn't want her to know, but because that's just not the relationship we have. But one day I felt a weird bump down *there*. My obvious first thought was that I must be dying. But, because I was still insured under my parents' plan, I had to go back to my childhood home to see a gynecologist, which led to the ultimate trap:

"Why do you need to see a gynecologist?" my mom asked. In her mind, a woman didn't need to go see the lady doctor until after she'd had sex.

I don't think I ever said the word *yes* or *no* when she asked me directly if I had "popped my cherry," and

I most definitely avoided the questions of virginity altogether. Whatever mumbo jumbo I said ultimately helped me land an appointment with the doc.

My first visit was uncomfortable, to say the least. The woman doing the exam was neither friendly nor informative, and I was left lying on the hard table with sweaty palms and a racing heart. She never even mentioned the bump, the one thing on my body that was keeping me awake at night and the only thing I'd been thinking about for weeks, so I had to ask. She looked at it for half a second with nonchalance. An ingrown hair, she said. It was an ingrown hair.

My weeks of terror thinking that I would soon shrivel away by cervical cancer dissipated with her quick glance and a pat out the door.

My next gyno appointment was an equally, if not more, horrific experience. Again, I thought there was something wrong with me, and again, the doctor side-stepped my concern. This time, though, I was overcharged for my visit and had to fight off wrongfully given bills for years.

It's true that, even now, years after those first experiences, I'm not super ecstatic when it comes to going to the lady doctor. I have flashbacks of having "the talk" with my mom, medical bills, and a brush with death-turned-ingrown-hair that fester in me like the common cold. I couldn't shake the bad feelings my experiences brought me, but I also couldn't not get a check-up.

After being on the fence about going back to the OB/GYN for a long time, l was finally pushed into action when a threatening conservative government gave me a small-handed nudge. Trump's administration was threatening to defund Planned Parenthood, criminalize abortion, and make women's health needs as difficult to obtain as possible. As much as l hated a cold metal scapula, l hated masculine bureaucratic control even more. l made an appointment with Planned Parenthood within that first month of the "defund" talk, and the first thing l did when l got there was cry.

l cried when l arrived at my appointment specifically because a very nice, tall, stocky security guard with a huge smile welcomed and escorted me in. Then l cried when l sat down inside because the woman who greeted me was so warm and kind.

l did not cry because I'm a female or hormonal or because I'm hypersensitive to warm, kind smiles. l cried because when that officer greeted me and the woman at the check-in smiled, l felt a sense of relief. l knew these people were there to protect and fight for everyone's basic right to choose whatever it is they want to do with their lives. l was so grateful for that and for them—and l was proud to be a part of it.

That was years ago, and recently, l finally had the nerve to go back into Planned Parenthood for my first exam in a while.

As always, l was nervous for my exam—sweaty palms, racing heart. The first thing the practitioner did when she walked through the door was smile and ask if I had any questions. She took a moment to listen about anything and everything going on and was kind enough to make a couple jokes to keep me calm. She let me ask all the questions I've ever had and answered them with intelligent, detailed answers. She performed the exam and explained everything to me, and before I left she took time to answer even more questions. She made me feel more knowledge-able about my own body and more comfortable taking advantage of different options I had to make choices that were right for me. And when I got back to the front desk to check out, I was told that under the wwc program, my exam was free—and for the second time in that office, I cried.

There are many things that I am grateful for, but one very big one is that I still have a place I can go where I'm greeted with warm smiles, valuable infor-mation, and people who are looking out for my well-being. A place where I can feel safe and where I can make the decisions that affect my entire life and future. I feel lucky to still have an organization and other area institutions that support my autonomy over my body. And if that means crying in a waiting room every once in a while, fine by me. Because who can say they've never done that anyway? I'm just lucky that they are tears of gratitude and pride, because you never know when everything will change.

How to:
Cry on Your
Mountain Bike

IT WASN'T LONG AGO that a commercial was circulating on Hulu that contained the storyline of an ordinary man on his Hero's Journey. The ad was for oat milk, but the man's agenda was to transform himself into a better person by waking up early every morning to go swim—and also to drink oat milk. Near the end of the thirty-second commercial, the music crescendoed in line with the man's triumph, and just as he held up the oat milk box in the swimming pool, I started to cry. Tears of pride and inspiration started dripping down my face while I watched this commercial, eating popcorn and drinking wine.

It's not that I'm overly sensitive. A few would even say I'm the opposite. They'd say I'm strong and resilient, and that's what I tell myself over and over when

I'm tearing up over an internet video of a dog being reunited with its owner. Or when I see people lined up on the streets fighting for the betterment of the long-standing, poorly treated underdogs.

I'm not a sensitive softy. I'm super tough and strong! I'm a rock! I'm steel, and I only let my emotions drip from my eyes when I'm in the safety of my own home with the blinds closed or hidden behind my sunglasses where no one can see me.

Or something like that.

Obviously I'm a little more soft than I let on, and when the world's weight started coming down during 2020's pandemic and political upheaval, my strong exterior metal shield cracked under the weight. Thus began the Year of Fuck It.

Fuck it, fine. I'm a big softie! Okay?!

The world's a shitfest party, and I'll cry if I want to.

But the one thing that helped me sort through the shitfest party and also made me cry more than puppy videos was mountain biking. During the entire year, the minute I got on my bike and started up a trail, all my thoughts would come out, streamlined in a way that was productive but also made everything very real. And so, many times I found myself on the trail, riding my bike and crying.

So, if you feel like going on a mountain bike ride to shatter your tough exteriors, dig in deep to your soft interiors, and sort out all the world's and your own personal problems, please feel free to take some tips from me first.

Crying Pro Tip #1: Do not cry while you ride uphill.

Crying while riding uphill is not a good idea. Which sucks, because riding uphill is best for thinking. Uphill is where everything slows down and you can sink deep enough into your thoughts and emotions to turn the eye faucets on. But beware, because something happens when you start to cry that they don't cover in anatomy class—your throat closes up. Like, your body decides that when water needs to come out your eyeballs, your throat can no longer pass air. Which is fine if you're sitting snug in your home, or on a slow walk with your dog. But when you are exhaustively exerting yourself up a mountain on a bike, you need that airway to be-the-fuck open to breathe.

Gasping for air on a slight incline is really trouble-some and unattractive, so wait until you're stopped somewhere—such as a beautiful meadow—and then you can start crying. Let that shit out.

Crying Pro Tip #2: Do not cry while going downhill either.

It's nearly impossible to cry downhill because you need to concentrate on the things that are coming up super fast. If you do get stuck crying downhill, trust me when I tell you to immediately pull over, because, much like a heavy sedative or trying to open your eyes while shampooing in the shower, crying makes every-thing really blurry and your eyes sting like hell.

Don't believe me? Try dumping your water bottle's contents in your face then bombing down a mountain with your eyes closed. That is what crying while riding downhill is. Good luck, sucker.

Crying Pro Tip #3: Pick the right trails.

I'm not always suffering up steep technical uphills and bomber downhills when I try to clear my head. The trails I cry on take only enough of my concentration to keep my mind from going haywire with all my pre-existing anxiety, but not enough that I can't still sort things out in a rational way.

If you do everything correctly, you'll get in a great rhythm. You'll ascend a trail while thinking about life and then descend to leave all those thoughts behind—just leave them up there at the top and never see them again.

The descent happens in a way that makes the world's problems fade into the trail. The shitfest of a bad day or year becomes a big drop on a sandy down-hill. The images of all the world's issues are contained within a techy rock crop. You'll never be able to navi-gate the depths of dramatic news stories on your own, but you can navigate a rock in the trail.

I can solve a problem on my mountain bike with a few tumbles and trials, but then I move on and there is nothing nuanced or convoluted about it. It's just a rock or a drop, and if I don't clean it, I will try again. And when I finally ride it, I will cry, because in a world where it feels like I can't do or fix anything else, I can at least ride down the trail and up the rocks.

Bravery

FOR A LONG TIME I had bravery all mixed up, and only recently did I figure out there is more than one way to be brave. The first way, the way I'm most familiar with, is a bold statement to the greater population that I don't care what anyone thinks. Not caring what anyone thinks helps abate fears of outside judgement and ridicule. It's not giving a rat's ass about what anyone says about you or your work. For a long time, I did this. I did it by turning off my emotions and closing my eyes, turning off the chatter of the world around me, and standing solitary, not giving a fuck.

While I was not giving a fuck about anyone else, I was also trying to do scary stuff outside. I was rock climbing for most of my twenties and mountain biking in between and this is, in a sense, the second way to be brave. Rock climbing and mountain biking are risky, and I knew these risks. I was pretty scared of heights, crashing, and death, and I knew how vulnerable I was hanging dozens of feet off the ground, or racing down a mountain, but I did it anyway. I calmed the chatter, quieted my beating heart, and focused on not freaking out and instead on being present.

I was present with what was in front of me, and for many years I lived this way, shutting off my emotions toward humanity and the people around me and becoming incredibly vulnerable while recreating outdoors. But I had it all mixed up. My relationships hit the ground and broke, and it took new relationships to realize that the most difficult thing in the world is standing in front of someone, or a group of people, knowing how vulnerable you are, but doing it anyway.

It took so long to realize that I'd gotten bravery mixed up. Being brave is being vulnerable with people. Being brave is keeping your heart open when you want so badly to close it. Being brave is taking a deep breath and sharing a soft moment with someone in front of you. Putting bravery in its rightful place has felt like starting anew—like learning how to be brave all over again. Day by day I set myself straight by trying to be vulnerable, open, and, whenever it's appropriate, not giving a fuck.

Karmic Cycle

ONE MORNING LAST WEEK, within the span of about fifteen minutes, my heart was shattered in two different ways: disappointment in humanity, and a great love for it.

It was an early Friday morning when I walked out of my downtown home to find someone had stolen the front wheel off my beloved bicycle. I've had bikes stolen before. I am no stranger to theft. But this time, for some reason, I was both sad and utterly annoyed. "Who would steal just one wheel?!" I whined to my coworkers when I went into the coffee shop where I worked. "What can you do with just one wheel?"

I was mad at the fact that whoever stole my front wheel didn't realize that my bike was my main mode of transportation and that in order for it to operate, it needed both wheels. Just as I was slamming my fist upon the counter with rage, one of the regulars at the coffee shop walked up to me.

"What happened?" he asked.

I told him about my bike wheel, and he gave me sincere sympathy, saying things like "That's too bad" and "What are you going to do now?"

I told him I'd have to buy a new one (bike riders know wheels are not cheap) and, without hesitation, this man pulled out the exact amount that I said I'd have to pay to buy a new wheel. He showed it to me—I laughed. He told me to have it—I thought he might be joking. He handed it to me and told me to go buy a new wheel. At that point I was so taken aback that I started mumbling and telling him things like "I couldn't sleep at night!" and "That's more than a day's worth of salary!"—even though I don't even make a salary.

Finally, he put the bill in my hand and calmly told me that my bike is obviously important to me and to go buy a new wheel so I can start riding again. With shaky hands and teary eyes, I accepted and gave him a hug.

I went to my other job that day in a complete daze. So many things happened within that very early morning. It made me think a lot about the concept of generosity and the responsibility that comes from it. The responsibility to do the right thing with the gift given to me, the responsibility to pay it forward, and the responsibility to show and feel gratitude toward this humbling experience. We are lucky enough to live in a town where this sort of thing happens, and it only happens because each of us makes it happen. He might not know it, but this man whom 1 know only from early morning lattes has made me think in a whole new light. 1 thank him for helping me out with my karmic cycle.

Getting Back on the Horse

MY FIRST DATE with Chris was on Friday the 13th in November, and on November 13 two years later, we broke up. Actually, it was late into the night of November 12 when I sat crying in his fake leather chair across the room from his emotionless expression, but I do believe that the clock's arms went past midnight when he said we would no longer work. He said we were too different and that he was holding me back. He liked working on his computer all day, I liked mountain biking. Neither of us could be happy, and so, on that November night, we decided to be momentarily, and greatly, unhappy instead.

I grieved for this relationship as much as anyone knows how to. I cried in bed, watched bad rom-coms, and sat around with my friends, drinking wine and questioning where it all went wrong. Where it went wrong, we concluded, were myriad issues, but we could make it all right by going to the mountains to clear our heads.

I had hardly gone mountain biking in the years I was with Chris, and I didn't even know how much that part of me was missing until I got back on the two-wheeled horse and pedaled up the trail and moved my body in a way that it was meant to.

My friends told me that I was meant to move on from my ex, and that "moving on" was making me go on a date. So that same day, while still on a mountain-biking high, I said yes to drinks with a stranger.

He was nice and bought me dinner at the Irish pub that Chris and I used to frequent for trivia night. Chris's ghost loomed everywhere, and I kept looking over my shoulder to see if he was going to walk in. Then I'd look back at the new man smiling in front of me and remember that I was pedaling forward, not back.

After we shared a few stories and a couple laughs, we walked outside and made loose plans to see each other again. As the to-do verbs floated up into the night sky, he pulled me in and kissed me. I didn't know it until then, but I was happy that after such a rocky road, I was finally pedaling forward and getting back on the horse.

The Economics
of Breakups

BREAKING UP is for the rich. If you are not, I would strongly suggest postponing a lover's split until you have gotten an extra job, saved up a good chunk of cash, or have been approved for a small business loan; investing financially in a relationship is just as important as investing emotionally.

In fact, after about the third date in a new relationship, it would be smart to open a new savings account titled in the name of your new special friend. Start depositing a sum of money into the account every time you and your partner quarrel. If you don't want a bank to be your relationship's third wheel, try hiding a stack of cash under a mattress instead. Either way, have some sort of savings set aside, because if you're going to freak out after a breakup, which will happen, it's good to do so responsibly.

Nothing is done responsibly after a breakup. In fact, the moment the words *This isn't working out* are muttered, the rational part of our brain turns off and the irrational side gets called up to the stage for an erratic flash dance. This flash dance is what makes you start buying everything you want and nothing you need, and it justifies itself by saying the word *need* to the guy behind the counter who is swiping your "emergency only" credit card for a triple-digit purchase mere hours after *Can we just be friends*.

Okay, maybe you really *do* need that brand-new jacket, but let me assure you—this is not an emergency.

An emergency is those I'm-back-on-the-market shoes you found on the internet just hours after you bought that jacket and just minutes after you opened that bottle of wine that you definitely need to dull the sting.

When the sting is dulled a little more, maybe you can also justify those new skis as an emergency. And the ski boots, climbing rope, and new climbing shoes that will finally and officially cut ties with your former significant other's gear closet.

You *need* all of it. You also need that second bottle of wine that helps with your newfound independent can-do go-getter attitude. Heck yeah. Now take a breath and make sure that you actually need these things. Yeah, you definitely do. And it's definitely an emergency.

How to:
Recreate Alone

DESPITE WHAT MY DOG thinks, I do have friends. And despite what my friends think, I won't die if I go do something outside by myself. Yes, the chances of me getting stuck somewhere with a flat bicycle tire or a twisted knee are higher, but I like to think I go solo responsibly. When I go it alone, either I tell someone where I'm going and how long I expect to be, or I go where there are plenty of other people around to check on me—or laugh at me—when I crash and/or find myself in need of assistance.

The fact of the matter is, I'm a bit of an introvert when it comes to recreation and asking people for accompaniment. I go on spontaneous lunch runs and bike rides, and very few of my friends are keen on going skiing/mountain biking/running *right now*. But, there is really no need to justify time outside alone, and in fact, I would highly encourage more people to try it out.

How to ski alone:

It was actually really difficult to convince myself to start skiing alone. Even the thought of driving to the mountain by myself kind of unmotivated me, but there came a time when I found myself in possession of a season ski pass and I was determined to use it.

Skiing alone at a ski resort is fine because you can just put on your helmet and goggles and lap your favorite runs and no one will recognize you. It's sort of like being invisible for a day, which works out great when you want to escape the world or when you yard sale on a blue right under the lift.

It's the lift line that can be a little more tricky on your ego since there is usually a specific line for singles, which just highlights to everyone that you are, in fact, a single. But when it's your turn, you can squeeze in with some new folks, which can go a few different directions: one, you're stuck with a group of friends (who are not your own) and you get to listen in on their sometimes interesting, but mostly heinous and meaningless, conversations; two, you're stuck with just one or two other people and no one talks to each other; or, three, and the most common scenario on a weekday, you're stuck with just one other person who also has weekdays off and an aversion to people and is also there alone. That person becomes your unofficial ski buddy for the rest of the day.

My ski buddies have included, but have not been limited to: over-sharers, proud and loose-lipped Texans, self-proclaimed Deadheads, vacationers, and outdoor gear experts. I've sat with pot-smoking kids and drunk teens, but most of the time, I have found that when you go skiing alone on a weekday, you will end up on the lift with an old retired guy.

These guys are super friendly and mean no harm. They are the ones who are more apt to mansplain things to you and also say something really inappropriate. It's okay, though, because they don't know any better—they're old men who are skiing alone on a Tuesday, just like you.

Not like you, though, the old men are there to reminisce with you and show off their skills from "the good old days" when "the snow used to be good" and they used to "race" or "live in Aspen" and were "semi-professionals back in their prime." "Not like these days when everything sucks," they all say. These men ski on a Tuesday to brag and to show off.

I, however, am there on a Tuesday for the sole purpose of *not* showing off. I am there to hide and listen to loud music, forget all my life's problems, make mistakes, learn from my mistakes, and look really stupid doing it without having to be embarrassed, impress anyone, or keep up with my bomber friends who look at me with pity when I'm last to show up at the lodge for beer. I am there to do whatever run I want however many times in a row I want and not have to explain myself to anyone.

No friends on a powder day, you say? I say no friends on a weekday.

How to mountain bike alone:

I started mountain biking alone around the same time I started skiing alone. Just like with skiing, I didn't really want to ride solo, but I was peer-pressured into it by my friends because they were tired of me not being able to mountain bike properly. Most of them suggested I ride by myself so that I could practice, and I was like, "Well fuck you too," and then we hugged and I continued to suck at biking.

I don't remember the exact day I mustered up enough courage to ride alone, but I do remember the trail I rode. It was an easy one that I'd done a million times before, but now that I was by myself I was lost. I could not find my own way on the trail. That was a very profound moment in my life, when I realized that I was not a leader like I'd always thought I was, but rather a follower, and a blind one at that. I'd been following my friends around on the trails all my life while I made conversation, asked them about their personal lives, and told them about mine. I never really looked at where our bikes were going. So when

I was out there on my own, I had to play dumb tourist and ask someone where I was—on my hometown trail. Luckily I was wearing a helmet and glasses that disguised me from anyone I might have known so that I could wobble my way to where I was supposed to be without too much shame.

I'll admit that I was scared the first time I biked alone. Any time I went over a technical section, I wondered what I would do if I crashed and didn't have anyone to save me. But then, like, fifteen mountain bikers passed from behind and they reminded me that I was not alone and that also I was very slow.

So, my advice for mountain biking alone? Stick with the aforementioned ski schedule. Go when the retired old guys go. Early in the morning or on week-days but preferably the combination. It's really the golden hour for all sports. And bonus with biking: you're not stuck on a chairlift with anyone, so you're less likely to hear stories about "the golden days in Aspen" or get mansplained to.

How to run or hike alone:

I never run with other people anyway because, dear lord, *why?* Why force someone to be with me when I'm at my worst. When I'm breathing heavily, red in the face, gross, and totally in my head thinking about how I can be a better me. So, yeah, my advice is to run alone. Always—or with a dog—it's the best way.

I don't love hiking alone, mostly because I don't love hiking, but sometimes I do it and more so these days because I've recently decided to take up fly fishing and the best fishing is up pretty creeks that generally require walking up trails to get to. Hiking alone is similar to running alone; it's a great time to think about bettering yourself or just about life in general. It's quiet and calm, so you can clear your head. That also means you can hear any crunch in the woods or creak of a tree. You can spot a bird and think it's a bear or you can spot a bear and think it's a crazy murder man. Hopefully the crazy murder man bear is just a friendly passerby, but to be honest, I don't want to be alone when I find out.

How to camp alone:

I try not to camp alone because I'm scared of crazy murder men and murder bears.

But when I do, I take all the precautions to keep myself safe, though these precautions probably won't actually keep me safe. I lock my tent's zippers together even though a simple sharp object such as a murder knife or murder claw could easily rip the entire tent to shreds, and I sleep with my dog who, instead of attacking murder man bears, will furiously wag his tail and ask for treats and pets. Mostly, I try to sleep inside a vehicle, which these days is the back of my truck with a topper that has a flimsy plastic side window and a broken back flap, neither of which locks. So, if you're like me and decide to camp alone in the peak of hunting season... in a notoriously huntable area... off a service road... make sure you have plenty of wine to help you fall asleep. It won't make you any safer, but it might make you feel less alone.

Brush the Snow Off

WHEN I WAS A KID I used to compete in downhill skiing, and by compete, I mean find the closest kid on the bunny slope at my hometown ski resort and challenge them to a downhill ski race.

I almost always won, at least that's how I remember it, but based on my current ski skill level, that could be questioned. After I had raced my share of bunnies, and I grew up a bit, my family stopped going to the resort so much and soon at all. I became a teenager and more interested in spending money on concerts and books than ski passes, and that mentality didn't change much even after I moved to a mountain town for college.

I blindly went through four years of college life without thinking twice about skiing, let alone racing strangers down bunny hills. Yet as I made a few friends, I noticed that people spoke an awful lot about The Mountain, which was, as you may have it, our local ski resort. They all made this mountain sound like some magical mecca in the clouds that I never actually saw in person and where everyone who's anyone goes whenever they can.

"Yeah, I went to the mountain this weekend. It was awesome," BroBra would say between shots of bad vodka and games of beer pong.

"Have you been yet?" he'd ask me. I'd fidget with my cup of warm PBR and think of a way to tell him that no—no, I had not. But I wouldn't tell him that because not attending The Mountain was very uncool in a mountain town, and so, leaning on my racing days on the bunny slope, I sugarcoated my abilities.

"Oh, I can totally ski! I grew up skiing!" I told BroBra. Then, years later, I told my new boyfriend the same thing when he asked me to go skiing with him.

It was early on in the relationship and I was still successfully hiding how significantly uncool I actually was. Until I could no longer hide it.

"There's something I need to tell you," I told him as we stood at the top of a very small hill that went to the chair lift.

The truth and my nervousness were coming out and I was trying to keep myself together while at the same time refreshing my memory on "pizza-ing" and "french fry-ing." I also needed to remain attractive, but my boyfriend was waiting for me at the bottom of the hill, so I took a deep breath, whispered to myself, "You totes got this," and slid forward. And then I fell down.

I slid down the non-steep hill toward where my boyfriend was staring at me in horror, and what I can only assume was embarrassment, as I was flailing around trying to get up. I don't know for sure, but I swear I saw him almost turn around to get on the chair lift without me.

"Yeah, it's been a few years," I admitted when I finally got myself upright and loaded onto the lift.

"I can tell," he said.

But his belief in me was (sort of) strong, and so we took the lift all the way up to the top where the adults skied and where there were runs labeled blue and green and black instead of "bunny slope" and had names like Demon and Exodus instead of Snowflake. I was either in heaven or in hell. It was too soon to tell.

I slipped and slid a few times but got my bearings and remembered how to turn my skis into different food shapes and as soon as my motor memory came back to me I took off.

I shot down the mountain as fast as I could, leaving my boyfriend in the dust, pizza-ing only when I was scared I was going too fast and bombing the rest of the way.

"Wow," he said when we got to the bottom. "You should really learn how to make turns."

"But that is not how you win a race!" I said as I took off with one big sweep of the skis and fell on my face.

A few months later, I went skiing with a friend and I felt confident enough to tell her I was ready for a steeper mountain on an epic pow gnar day. She was also confident in my abilities and a lot more patient when I did not live up to said abilities.

"TURN! TURN!" she yelled at me through blizzard conditions.

In order to save my life, I did what she said. I pushed my toes and I cranked my heels and I started floating up over the snow and slowly down the mountain. I couldn't stop giggling and squealing the entire way down, and when I got to the bottom of the hill, I brushed the snow off, looked at my friend, and challenged her to another downhill race.

For All
the Ones
We've Lost

I'VE LOST THREE FRIENDS to avalanches. That number might not seem like a lot to some and it might seem like a lot to others, but it's too many. The truth is, the number could easily be higher and I'm grateful it's not, but I do become more nervous during the winter when the snow is unstable. Every time someone calls my phone, I think, *Another one lost*.

My friend Luke called me late December 2020 to tell me our friends Jeff and Bert had just died in an avalanche. They went skiing in a nearby area that they knew well and luck and fate all went wrong and they didn't survive. Their bodies were recovered, but so many of their family and friends will not.

I received the news as anyone would probably expect. My brain took a minute to even connect the dots, and then I gasped out, "What about Kristi? Has anyone spoken to her?"

Kristi is Jeff's wife and my former roommate and friend. She is also the brand-new mother to their twin boys, whom Jeff loved very much. I wailed out in pain for her, a mother of two and now a widow.

The news of Jeff's and Bert's deaths came on a Saturday. By Sunday I had already called, texted, or emailed everyone I knew who knew them, seeking out ways I could help. I'd contacted friends I hadn't talked to in months or years. I connected with people I didn't even know.

"How is she? What can I do?" I was asking all of them. The only person I realized I hadn't asked was Kristi.

The thing with death is that it throws everything off kilter. Your normal everyday patterns are disrupted and you're left in a cloud of unknown—even if you've already experienced death, it always feels new and uncharted every time it happens. I never know what to do whenever I learn that someone close, or someone I know—even just a little—dies. Mostly I just freeze. I grieve alone and hide from any consequential situation because I think I'll do or say the wrong thing.

I think that saying "I'm sorry" isn't enough and "How are you?" is too much. "What can I do?" feels empty. So does "I'm here if you ever need anything."

Kristi was probably falling apart—who wouldn't be after losing their husband and father to their newborn twins?—but she is also one of the strongest, most self-sufficient humans I know, and that, somehow, made it harder for me to reach out to her. Almost like I'd be denying or questioning her ability to survive something hard. Like it was my duty to trust that she would be okay, that *she's got this*.

I took a walk in the evening after the avalanche on top of a hill looking down at Kristi's and Jeff's house. I stood there for so long in the cold winter dusk, and I cried silently for both of them and everyone who knows them and for Bert and everyone who knows him. I couldn't come up with the right things to say or do. I couldn't bring myself to ring her doorbell with a lasagna and flowers. But, however small the gesture, I finally sent an *I'm sorry* text and hugged her and our friends at the memorial while we shared an afternoon to remember all the ones we've lost.

Cold Coffee

ON THE MORNING of October 31, two days before the 2020 presidential election and during a full moon, multiple planetary retrogrades, and a global pandemic, I decided to quit coffee cold turkey. Not just coffee, mind you. I decided that I had to extract all caffeine from my life, simply because my supply ran dry.

I'd already kind of been thinking about quitting caffeine, but that Halloween morning, I opened my cabinets to find only an empty bag of coffee, so I shrugged, got back under a blanket, and googled all the terrible withdrawal symptoms that someone who's been drinking coffee since high school could expect.

I found warnings about headaches, fatigue, low energy, irritability, anxiety, poor concentration, depressed mood, and tremors. I thought that all sounded pretty similar to how I was already feeling during 2020 and, more prominently, the days entering the presidential election. So I thought, *What the heck, let's do this.*

The next few days were interesting. I found myself staring at a lot of walls. I once caught myself staring at a bird for, like, fifteen minutes and daydreaming about how cute it was bouncing around looking for food and hoping it was happy and warm.

Daydreaming became my number one hobby for my cold turkey journey. Many times I drifted off thinking about what my life would be like without my caffeinated love—my former life's blood. Not in a nostalgic *I'll miss it* kind of way, but in a reinventive way. Like, what kind of *person* would I be without coffee? Would I be super cool and super chill, no longer anxious? Would I be an herbal-tea-drinking yogi who wears flowy skirts, eats raw, and says things like *namaste* and *rad*? Would I own a matching tea set and china? Would I start eating tiny crustless finger sandwiches at high noon?

All these things were crossing my caffeine-less foggy mind while the world was imploding around me: the nail-biting election, the COVID-19 pandemic, and worry about all the what-ifs. And while I was lamenting the future of our country—and also wondering how you would make tiny crustless finger sandwiches—I kept losing track of what daily activity I was in the middle of, or I would set something important down somewhere and immediately forget what and where it was.

It was as if I were walking through a dream, watching the country balance on a precarious tilting point. I thought the smartest thing to do was to go out, get some fresh air, and get my blood flowing, so on day number four without caffeine, I went on a mountain bike ride.

Of course, when I got to the trail I realized I'd forgotten everything. I left my water bottle and phone at home, and I'd improperly dressed myself because I didn't have enough bandwidth to figure out what the temperature outside would be.

While I rode my bike, I felt like I was both high on drugs and hung over; my head hurt and everything around me moved really slow. I didn't, though. I went fast, and even though I was bouncing downhill on some technical rock, I was still thinking about how cute birds are and also about electoral votes and why some states were taking so long to count theirs.

Then I crashed. Naturally.

I probably should have seen it coming, but the tumble was slow enough not to do any damage and just left me a bit bloody and bruised.

When I made it back down the trail to my truck, what I saw was not the blood from my knee. In my stupor, I saw the way the evening fall light was hitting the tall grass in the meadow in front of me. The world is beautiful and also burning in flames. And that's what it feels like to quit coffee cold turkey.

Doom Scrolling

If ANYONE ASKS ME where I was on a day that an important event in history happened, I can pretty confidently give a blanket answer of "I was staring at my computer." If it happened within the past five or so years, I was probably breathlessly scrolling through my news feeds, devouring numerous articles and chomping down on long lists of comments made by people whose education background was the Hogwarts School of Witchcraft and Wizardry.

So, I bet you can guess where I was right before the 2021 presidential inauguration, on Wednesday, January 6, 2021, when a buncha flag-waving toothless furries stormed our nation's capital. I can't even tell you how brightly my face glowed against the electromagnetic blue rays of my computer. I needed coverage of the coverage: every point of view, every word of mouth, every student of Professor Albus Dumbledore.

No wonder I forgot to eat lunch. I was busy eating other people's opinions.

At the eleventh hour of my breaking point, I stopped. Mostly because my dog needed a walk, but also because I realized I was rereading the same articles over and over. I had educated myself on the event hours before, and now it was just speculations and opinions that honestly didn't really matter. What good would it do to know that Melania Trump was looking at rugs during the attack, how Donald responded to the insurrection on Twitter, what that guy's tattoo meant and why his teeth were missing? I stopped reading because I already knew.

I already knew that Melania didn't care and that Trump instigated the violence, and I am pretty sure I know why that guy's teeth were missing. I've known these things since 2016, and frankly I'm getting bored reading about it. What I'd like to read about is action and change.

Before that happens, though, we all keep doom-scrolling the internet because it is super addicting and, honestly, it's kind of exciting. We all want to be on the front lines of the circus crash; we are all fast-news rubberneckers at heart.

Yes, the internet can be useful and informative. So many good things can be found, but right now the internet is oozing with as many toxins as that self-sabotaging drama-addict friend who endlessly complains about everything and won't do anything about it—and girl, I'm up to my ears hearing about your drama. Perhaps it's time to find a professional to talk to.

Hopefully soon, though, the internet, along with the United States, can find a wonderful therapist or just focus a little better on the matters at hand. But in the meantime, may we all intelligently inform ourselves, take action when we can, and then lightly step away from the glowing electromagnetic radiation of our personal devices.

The Boyfriend Belay

I'VE BEEN SPORTING for most of my life. I started to ski when I was five and started riding a bike when I was six. My go-tos as a twelve-year-old were running track, rollerblading, and jumping rope. At some point I started snowboarding but did not stick with it, just like I didn't really stick with kickflips and ollies on my skateboard—but damn it if I didn't spend hours upon hours in my garage trying.

College introduced me to mountain biking, rock climbing, beer pong, and running from the cops. I spent sunny weekends at local crags scraping myself up against rock walls simply because my friends were doing it, and I went on my first mountain bike ride for the same reason.

My mantra was that I would, for the most part, try anything once. I would usually try pretty hard at something, too, but when I saw that I wasn't getting any better, I would switch sports. It happened often because I've never really had an affinity for athletics—I was more of a book nerd—and though I loved being outside and doing things there, I never caught onto recreation very quickly.

I see that this can be perceived as greatly annoying and a huge personality flaw—I most definitely come off as a quitter, a flake, or more likely a poser—but let's face it, I was never going to become the next Toni Hawk anyway, so why not try my hand at... well... *everything*?

When I graduated college, I found my outdoor résumé embarrassingly full of holes. It could have set me up for a lifetime of sporting success, but instead, it landed me in my twenties as a mountain-town barista who overused the statements "Yeah, I used to do that" and "I'm not very good." My nostalgia for all those fun things was getting heavy, so finally in my late twenties I decided I had to cut the crap and focus on just one or two sports. I had to focus on my follow-through.

The impetus for my newfound focus was bolstered by the anger I'd accumulated from a breakup. I had been dating a climber who both expedited my growth in climbing and stunted it with his desire to always lead the routes and with his liberal use of the "boyfriend belay." He would casually pull the rope tighter whenever he saw I was struggling or when I kindly asked him to. When we broke up, my goal was to dismantle all of these crutches and become my own independent climbing woman. I bought a rope, called up my girl friends, and promised them I'd be leading all our climbs by the end of fall. This goal was ambitious and also a slap-in-the-face lesson in focusing and following through on these heady promises. I no longer had a boyfriend to help pull me up over a crux and then give me a kiss when I couldn't even finish the route. Instead, I had girl friends who held me accountable both physically and metaphorically to get me over the crux and up to those anchors. There were no "it's okay" kisses if I didn't make it.

I more or less quit climbing after that. Maybe it was because my focus wasn't strong enough to get over the mental crux of leading climbs, but also, after a certain age or amount of time, we all start losing our climbing partners. After all my friends started to move away or have families that took up their free time, I started mountain biking more because I could do that alone and whenever I wanted. No one was around to force me to do something I didn't want to do or try anything that scared me, and after an entire season of becoming a pro hike-a-biker, I realized that that was not a good thing. I was my own crutch. In fact, I was giving myself the boyfriend belay without even having the boyfriend.

When I turned thirty, I was on a mountain bike ride when I realized I was giving myself the boyfriend belay not just in biking, but in all walks of life. Just like my list of unaccomplished attempts at outdoor sporting, I had jumped around houses, relationships, and jobs any time things got hard. My list of months-long employment was long because I either got bored easily or just didn't want to get over that crux when the job started to get less fun and interesting. Why work so hard at something if I don't think it's worth it in the future? Why not just take the easy way out: get off my bike and walk around the hard parts? Ultimately, what happened that day in my thirties was that I got tired of getting off, on, off, and back on my bike. Tired of rewriting my résumé. Tired of starting all over again. It was more exhausting to stop and go than it was to just push through. So on one of my favorite trails at a spot I would have normally stopped and gotten off my bike to walk around the big rock crop, I just pushed through. When I did, my bike seized in the rock gaps and my pedals stopped moving, but I just chanted *keep going keep going keep going*, and I pushed through it to the end. Pushed through even after it got hard, pushed through even after I got stuck, and when I got to the other side, I gained back my momentum and kept pedaling, further and stronger.

How to:
Speak Bro

THE LANGUAGE-LEARNING APP Duolingo has shown me that I can learn a variety of languages: Romanian, Irish, Klingon, and High Valyrian—the official language of *Game of Thrones*. However, Duolingo is missing one language I sometimes wish I knew: the language of Bro.

Bro was the official second language of my college, a college known for its bro-ness. The outdoor recreation scene dominated the campus, as did smoking marijuana—a pastime for which we became nationally infamous. Many of my college friends spoke various dialects of Bro, mostly High Bro but also Drunk Bro and Everyday Bro. I wanted to be able to communicate with them, so I started to pick up a few words here and there. I heard it spoken mostly in the school hallways, but sometimes out in the wild, too: parties, outdoor trails, at the bars as the bros came in, après-ski. Over time and through observation, I found that the secret to learning Bro was to engage as the bros do, taking shots of Fireball and shotgunning PBRs over games of beer pong, or just standing around a dirty coffee table. This helped me fit in with the bros and also helped me, in my drunken state, to become more confident in speaking their language.

I continued to learn by total immersion. I went where the bros did, usually mountain biking, near ski resorts, and hanging around seedy bars, and that's how I found out that Bro is a heavily auditory language. It is mostly comprised of low-pitched aggressive giggles, grunting, a bit of yelling, and deep, guttural outbursts of laughing. When asked a question, a bro will use a single syllable noise for an answer, oftentimes followed by a giggle or a shrug. If that bro has a bro-buddy around, the second bro will help the mono-syllabic bro out by bro-splaining his own answer to the question. Bros tend either to agree quickly with each other's answers or to disagree so loudly that the Bro language becomes slurred and punctuated with emotion.

The language of the Bros is both complicated and uncomplicated, because at first, you don't really know what it all means: the noises, the grunts, and the giggles. Once you get the hang of Bro language, though, you know that most of what is being said is just

"That is/was really cool and/or very impressive." Once you understand that, the language of the Bro becomes a lot less intimidating to learn, because you'll probably never say anything wrong or offend anyone. Just stay excited about everything all the time and poof, there you have it—you don't need Duolingo—congratulations, you are fluent in Bro.

How to:
Not Say Sorry

A FRIEND OF MINE recently made the resolution to stop saying sorry so much. The word seems to be common in our female gender pack, and we tend to apologize more often than we should for things that we maybe never did.

Women say sorry for being too loud, and for being too quiet. We say sorry for being driven, successful, and strong. And for feeling sad, tired, or weak.

Heck, we oftentimes say sorry for saying sorry.

I personally tend to apologize for being clumsy, forgetful, and tall. And for the fact that sometimes I work a lot. I apologize on behalf of my dog, on behalf of my opinions, and for making bad jokes. When I get annoyed, sad, or hangry, I say sorry—especially for the latter. Sometimes even when someone does something nice for me, I apologize. Just the other day, a very nice gentleman bought me a beer and I apologized to him for not paying for it myself.

Who does that?

Females do. Heck, HUMANS do. We do it for various reasons and so, whether my friend's non-apologizing resolution was intended to make a worldly feminist statement, or just to clean up her conversations, I commended her on her decision.

I told her I supported her and then I wished her good luck.

I wished her good luck not to be cavalier or sarcastic, but in an actual "good luck with that" sort of way because I, too, have tried going the "sorry not sorry" route and it ended terribly.

I chose not to say sorry when I knew nothing was my fault and I ended up with the short end of a pretty bad stick. I was expected to say sorry even though I had nothing to be sorry for. I was punished for it and for that, I was sorry. So, what I meant when I told my friend good luck was, "Good luck, I hope you're not sorry when you're not sorry." And then I'm almost positive that I said sorry, and then said sorry for saying sorry.

RBG and the F-word

I HAD A FIVE-PERSON Zoom meeting with four men the other day. That's four men and me discussing business, which really meant that it was a four-person Zoom meeting: four men discussing business. I, on the other hand, sat muted, listening to the men exchange ideas about a work project that I was supposedly taking the lead on.

I listened to them talk about my project until I unmuted myself to speak on my own behalf, and when I tried, the men spoke over me and made a couple jokes until my stuttering and hand-raising became background noise and my Zoom window faded out and off the screen.

When I thought I'd disappeared completely, I started to put my hair up. And that's when, for the first time, I heard my name. Finally, all eyes were on me.

"Look, we can all watch her fix her hair!" one of them said. Then they laughed and laughed and waited for my expected response meant to entertain them.

The best I could do was give a thumbs-up, which made the men laugh even more, and then I waited for them to finish so we could wrap up the meeting and I could start being productive again.

When my screen went black after the call, I was trying not to get mad. I couldn't be mad because of the four men. I would put my money on it that they'd all identify as feminists. Or at least, if they were up against a firing squad, they would swear to heaven and hell that men and women should have an equal voice in all Zoom meetings. I guarantee that they'd step up to the guillotine plate and tell the executioners that they thought I, too, as a woman, deserved a chance. I really believe they would, but instead, in one way or another, they muted me.

A few days after yet another man-jority muted Zoom call, the Honorable Justice Ruth Bader Ginsburg died, and I just crumbled. I cracked and shattered. Everything in my heart and soul hurt, and I was sad and terrified all at the same time. It's actually amazing how someone you don't know can affect you so deeply, but when she died it felt like she was the last and only person on this earth who was able to crawl into my computer and hit that unmute button. The last person who could have said, "Excuse me, gentlemen, please stop noticing her hair and listen to what she has to say."

Please shut up and let her talk. Listen to her thoughts and ideas and stop noticing her gender. Listen to her needs and rights. Please stop citing your religion and, instead, cite her body as her own. Take note of her and her situation and her life and make them just a little bit easier by not forcing her down. Make them mean something; make them matter.

RBG had the ability to take the words and pleas spoken over and over by women—words that have beaten the dead horse—and make the words matter. She sat shoulder to shoulder, face to face with the men who wanted to mute her, and she smiled, ignored their laughter, and made laws instead. So when she died in the sea of men, in the hurricane of what is our current political climate, my blood ran cold and my hope for feminism grew thin.

The word *feminist* in itself is triggering—if I were to put it on my online dating profile I'd lose more potential suitors than the Rump has lost marbles. The word is interchanged with *anti-men* or *angry woman*; oftentimes both because they go hand in hand.

Apparently, a feminist is a woman who hates men and screams about it all the time. A feminist takes extreme and sometimes violent actions that are hysterical and disruptive. A feminist, they say, is—

ironically—very masculine. A feminist is loud, stubborn, and closed off. But that is not a feminist. Those things are just characteristics of some people in an ocean of a lot of different kinds of people.

Being a feminist doesn't mean that I hate everything that signifies "male." It actually doesn't mean that I hate anything. Granted, I'm not too fond of number 45, Mitch McConnell, Kyle Rittenhouse, or the guy who stands in front of our local Planned Parenthood every day with a picket sign, but I don't hate them just because they're men. I hate them because they're racists, murderers, and literally running our livelihoods into the burning ground. Also, trying to stop me from getting affordable female health care. I hate that.

I'm not forcing anyone to be less of a man so I can be more of one. I enjoy wearing skirts and flirting with boys. Some of my favorite nights are snuggling with a glass of wine and popcorn to watch the long list of rom-coms that Netflix recommends to me. I cry when I'm happy, and I squeal when I see a cute puppy. But if I ride my bike faster than a man, have an opinion about anything, or pull the trigger on a joke before a guy does, it doesn't mean I'm trying to make him feel bad about himself. It simply means that I'm good at riding bikes and I'm funny.

On the day RBG died, we lost a female voice that people listened to. She didn't let herself be muted just because she was challenging or intimidating. No one called her "nasty," although our then-president did say she was too small. No one said she was out of her mind or called her a fucking bitch. No one suggested she work on her anger management problem then go to a good old-fashioned movie. RBG was the kind of feminist who hit the unmute button on our country's Zoom call and said, "Excuse me, gentlemen, we have something to say," and no one said a thing about her hair.

What's Happening

I WORK FOR a newspaper that requires me to, once a week every week, deliver newspapers to businesses around town. No, I don't get to yell out "Extra extra! Read all about it!" while riding around on my bicycle, because, even though I have the job of a ten-year-old boy, I am a grown woman. So, instead, I drive around in my car and quietly place stacks of newspapers inside business buildings where they belong.

This is a fairly monotonous job that I do mostly in silence because it doesn't take a lot of talking to be a newspaper-delivering ninja. In fact, the less chit chat, small talk, and pleasantries, the better. But once a week, every week, one particular business employee kills my ninja flow.

"What's happening," he always says.

Mind you, he says this. It's not quite a question, yet still inquisitive enough to interrupt my flow and force me to pause for a second.

What IS happening? I have to think to myself.

I'm snapped out of my head and forced to truly reach deep down inside to ask myself how to answer this absurd non-question.

"Good" is what I eventually land on.

But *good* is not the appropriate response, and my answer is wrong, and for some reason this angers me.

HOW'S it going? I feel the urge to correct him and fill him in on global small-talk rules and social norms, but I don't because I am not a pedant. I am a newspaper ninja.

So I protest for the next few months by answering his "what's happening" with "good," hoping that he'll catch on and change his ways.

He doesn't, though, and our game of question/answer chicken went on until early summer when I was feeling particularly sassy and thought I'd accept his dumb question-statement. So I prepared myself to answer correctly this time.

When I got to the door of the liquor store that day, the butterflies ramped up in my stomach and I puffed out my chest with pride for knowing what was actually *happening*.

"What's happening," he sang out.

"Oh, just delivering papers!" I responded gleefully. I nailed it. I finally answered his stupid non-question, but what I got from him was silence.

He didn't even respond. I left the store frustrated that he didn't even care what was happening, he didn't actually want to know, he sucked and so did everyone else.

Then the next week came around.

"What's happening," he said on cue.

Well, if you must know, I just broke up with my boyfriend, my best friend just moved away. I'm broke, I'm sick, I stubbed my toe on the way to work yesterday, and my car is making a funny noise. Also, our government is going to shit, the environment is going to shit, I myself am going to shit, kids are saying things like "lit" and "woke" to me, and my dog keeps running away.

Of course I didn't actually say that out loud, because I finally found the correct answer:

"Nothing," I mumbled and walked out the door as swiftly as I came in.

Making
a Spectacle

I'VE NEVER BEEN a huge fan of clubs. Anything that involves raising my right hand and pledging my allegiance makes me queasy. I've failed multiple times at book clubs, and gym memberships make my palms sweaty, so the worst thing that might happen to me is being *forced* into a club.

But I was. I was forced into the glasses club. Not fine stemware, but the kind of glasses that create one more wall between you and your vision of the world.

At twenty-nine I'd never had an issue with my sight. I was proud of my 20/20 eyesight like I was proud of my talent for perfectly cooked pasta or my ability to lip-sync to the Spice Girls.

At thirty, though, my eye-pride dissipated and I was left with blurred disappointment.

It happened in one day during the fall—not "one day during the fall"—no, it was IN one day during the fall. I was in the desert on a camping trip reading a book one evening, and wallah, the next day I could no longer clearly see the words.

Contrary to what I thought, or what the internet told me when I googled "sudden loss of vision," I did not have a stroke, diabetes, aneurysm, or brain tumor. What I did have was a phenomenon my optometrist unapologetically called "getting older." After a few tests, she agreed that I had indeed lost my 20/20 vision, gave me a certificate of nearsightedness, and welcomed me into the glasses club.

The weeks after that were literally eye-opening. Not only could I see again, but I also, being inducted into the club, experienced a culture that I'd never known.

The glasses club is sort of secret, but everyone knows about it. It's like Fight Club in that no one talks about it, but unlike it in that we can't all be or look like Brad Pitt (who, FYI, is also part of the glasses club, but we don't talk about it). I instantly felt a secret comradery toward other eyeglass-wearers, and the first time I took my dog on a walk with my glasses on, I felt myself giving a slight nod and grin to any other quadra-eyed passerby. Whether they noticed or reciprocated is unknown, because I was still having trouble with my peripheral vision, but it felt good to be amongst potential friends.

As I spent more time in the club, I started noticing that I was becoming *that* person. Saying things like "I can't read this, where are my glasses?" and then putting on my glasses and saying "Ah, now that's better." I was doing things I always saw other people do, like squint, take off my glasses, rub them with a cloth, squint at them, and then put them back on. Or continuously push the frames back up the bridge of my nose when they would slowly slide down. It's not being a nerd; it's being a part of the club.

One day I learned a big lesson about the club. I was walking downtown when a rainstorm broke loose. No one except members of the quadra-eye-club could have warned me what that walk was going to be like. Two rain-sodden blurry pieces of glass in front of my eyes made my seven-block walk feel like I had taken acid and stepped into the ocean. About half-way through my aquatic journey, I looked up to see a gentleman also walking through the storm with glasses, and all I wanted to do in that moment was yell out my sympathies to him while doing a running high-five jump, but we would have missed hand contact because neither of us was able to see. Instead, I smiled at him as much as I could muster before continuing my journey into the blurry unknown.

Dear Sir

I KNOW I'M GETTING SPAM EMAILS when they are addressed to Sir, but mostly I know it's spam when they address me as Jenna—sometimes Jen, oftentimes Jenny. I imagine this happens because people, and their computers, can't quite grasp my real name, which is Jennaye.

Jennaye also generates a red squiggly line when typed out. Computers will often autocorrect it to Janine, Janet, or Jennifer. All great names, none of them mine.

One is, however, my sister's name. Yes, my mother named us Jennifer and Jennaye, which has always caused befuddlement and anguish in our household. Unfortunately, my sister is older than me, so she took dibs on Jen and Jenny as nicknames and also the bigger bedroom. I was societally stuck with Jane. Or, Jenna, or Joanna.

By middle school, I was fed up with intervening as flustered teachers tried pronouncing my name in front of the classroom every new school year, so I started calling myself Nicole.

Nicole is my middle name and also an easy way for middle school boys to call me "nic hole." So in high school I went back to Jennaye. My schoolmates did not get the memo, though, which just made the whole situation worse.

"Who's Jennaye?" the Nic Hole boys would say when I was called on in class. So then I had to go back to correcting people on both the pronunciation *and* my *actual* name.

It got better after college when I finally heard through the grapevine about another Jennaye, spelled Janae. Although I never met her, she suddenly became my ally in this world. We were struggling together to defend this name that computers and people everywhere thought was wrong. It was an oddly gratifying moment when I heard about her, like, *Yeah, see? That's right, my name is a real name because someone else has it, too.*

But just because someone else has my name doesn't mean that it's any less difficult for people to pronounce or spam emails to get correct.

I still get the "Dear Jen" emails and the "Dear Sir" ones, because Jennaye is that confusing for people.

But I'd rather not spend my life correcting people I'll probably never see again, and I don't have the time to reply to the spam emails: "Sorry, I do not want to sign up for your insurance, and by the way, my name is Jennaye. Please update your files." I can just continue being Janine or Jen to that guy I met once, and I will keep smiling whenever he says hello.

White Whale

THERE IS A DOWNHILL SECTION of a local mountain bike trail that sends my heart into my throat for reasons I can't truly specify. The trail's not more dramatic than anything I usually ride. It's steep, but not too steep. It's technical, but not too technical. It's sandy, but not enough to bog me down. Years of mountain biking later, though, I still stop my bike at the top of this section because my nerves overtake me every time.

The problem is, I know it too well. I've been riding that trail since I was practically a beginner, and the first time I tried going down I panicked and crashed and so it permanently scared me. But it's a section I have to conquer. I must have it—it has become my white whale—or so it became known to me and my friends.

I stare it in its eyes, I talk to it, I even taunt it some-times. I try to woo it into submission, hoping it'll hear me out and be easy on me, but nothing changes; a whale is a whale. So almost every week, when I start getting closer to the whale, I talk to myself:

It's okay, you got this. You got this. Just do it. You got this. Elbows out, butt back, knees out, you got this.

Then, when I see the first rock drop, I hold my breath and I creep up to its edge:

Nope nope nope nope nope, you don't got this. And I stop, get off my bike, get mad at myself for not gotting this, and walk back up the hill to try it again.

I session this hill so many times I exhaust myself just from hiking up with my bike, and I shame myself for not being able to conquer my whale.

There is something to be said about that little voice in my head, though. The one that says, *You're better than this. You've done much harder things. This is below your ability level. You've got this!*

So last week, I looked my white whale in the eye, cranked up some inspiring music through my head-phones, held my breath, and did it.

I hooked my white whale. Butt back, knees out, heart stopped, I rode down that section that had been keeping me awake at night. The section that I spent way too long and too much energy on. And when I got to the bottom, I yelped loudly and cried.

Pride, happiness, relief, all wrapped up into one white whale.

When I was done celebrating, I looked back up the hill and noted how manageable those rock drops and sandy spots looked from that perspective. That white whale wasn't so big and scary after all, so I walked back up and I rode it again.

Wonder What iPhone Is Best? The One iHave

WHEN PEOPLE MARVEL at the antiquity of my cellphone, I say, *Yeah, it's an iPhone 1* when in actuality it could be an iPhone 2 or 3 or 4—I can't know for sure, because nowhere in or on the phone does it identify itself.

You, tech-savvy reader, want to check for yourself. You think you know more than me because you've owned all the iPhones and you know all the secret tabs and lists and buttons, and yes perhaps you do, but trust me, nowhere have I found on my iPhone where it says "iPhone 1." Or 2 or 3 or 4.

But whether it is an iPhone 1 or 100, it is the best phone on the market—that is, if it is still on the market—and here is why:

The iPhone 1 is free.

I received my iPhone 1 from my friend Stacy. She saw the abomination of my very cheap smart-ish phone that had lived snugly in my back pocket since about 2006, and she snickered and said, "Guuurrllll, you need a new phone!" And then she looked with great pity upon my dumb smartphone with a sadness I couldn't comprehend.

The next time I saw Stacy she handed me an iPhone 1 because, like the rest of the world, she was on to number seven. It had a chipped phone case that looked like it came from the sixties, because it did, and when she placed the phone in my hand, I felt more like a progressive grown-up than I ever had.

"You can just have it," she said.

I kissed her feet and then bought her a case of beer to thank her. So I guess the iPhone 1 isn't technically free. It costs one case of beer.

You can still get buy-back money for it on the Apple website.

The moment I found out that my new old iPhone was truly indistinguishable as an iPhone 1, 2, 3, or 4 was when I became curious as to how much it was worth. This is due to the fact that only days after Stacy gave me the iPhone 1, I started getting comments from friends that went something like "Guuurrllll, you need a new phone!"

Even though in my eyes I just got a new phone, I thought they might have a point. This led me to wonder if this relic was worth anything and that maybe the value of it had actually gone up over time. Was that a thing yet? Old Apple products gaining in value with age? So I *Antiques Roadshow*'d that shit.

"Get up to $260 in credit toward a new iPhone. Just trade in your eligible smartphone," Apple's website said.

Then the website asked me to pick which iPhone I wished to trade in, and that is when I discovered my iPhone had no name.

I spent a long time trying to find its identity through the deep caverns of the phone and also Google searches, and after giving up, I chose the oldest one on the list.

"Your phone is worth: $1," Apple's website said and then iPunched me in the face.

The hopes of becoming a trazillionare for owning the oldest working and perfect iPhone ever had dissipated, but in retrospect, it is still $1 net gain. Unless you count the cost of the beer I gave Stacy, which I don't.

It's simple.

After finding out that my iPhone I is monetarily worthless, I decided to keep it around. I learned about things called "apps" and taking pictures and what "using data" meant. I was eons behind basic smartphone knowledge but grateful for friends, tweens, babies, and grandparents who were helping me to learn about things like "emoticons," which apparently are actually called emojis.

It's indestructible.

Cell phones might be our fifth limb but, just like everything else that isn't actually physically attached to me, I drop it a lot.

My phone has hit dirt and seen the inside of the toilet bowl, and then a rice bowl and then a toilet bowl again—more rice—and a river—more rice. I've left it in the direct July sun for more than three hours but less than twenty-four, and at one point the chipped psychedelic-colored case fell off and it has been naked ever since. Through all that, I can proudly say that my iPhone 1 is still alive and well. I can't even say that about my sunglasses, ChapStick, or the pair of strappy sandals I wore to a wedding in Denver that I owned a week before they tore and I lost one. In fact, the iPhone 1 is probably the thing I've owned the longest without breaking, and it might just be the perfect companion; it stays by my side wherever I go and through whatever I put it through. When I accidentally leave it somewhere, no one will steal it because no one wants it. It listens to me while I talk at it and never gets angry even when I fling it across the room because I accidentally left it on top of a towel that I snatched up and I finally break its screen.

So, for all these reasons, thank you, iPhone 1. You are simple, you are indestructible, you are perfect, and iLove you.

Baby Fever

WHEN I WAS A YOUNG naive lady in my twenties, I was obsessed with a boy named Tyler. Tyler, on the other hand, was obsessed with kids. He was an aspiring teacher who coached a high school soccer team and he babysat his nephew *for fun*. And I was having a lot of fun with no children around.

Even though I wasn't a fan of the youth, I still took a nannying job to try to get myself to like kids so Tyler could try to like me. But at the end of the day, the only things those whippersnappers were good for were their leftover dinosaur-shaped chicken nuggets and their quirky, but entertaining, TV shows.

A few years later, after Tyler exited the picture, I met Tall Dark and Handsome, who actually came equipped with two kids. After a couple years of dating, I blindly decided to live with all three of them, if only for the cheap rent and dinosaur nuggets. Four blissfully chaotic months of school lunches, homework, and screaming fights between siblings, and I moved out.

Now in my thirties, my only life goals are to find affordable rentals, land a job that doesn't kill my soul, and have meaningful savings in my bank account. I also wish to someday have health insurance, although last I checked, no plan covers the inevitable "baby fever" I will supposedly get when my "clock starts ticking."

Even though I don't want kids, I do want to date and someday possibly get married. I'd like to be a part of a small family consisting of me, my sterile husband, and a couple of pets. I don't think that just because I don't want to bring little peanuts into the world that I should have to die alone.

And so I date. But trying to date in a world of an average 1.9 kids per household is not easy when you would like to average zero kids in your household, and I haven't quite figured out how to broach the subject to my potential suitors.

"I enjoy reading and taking my dog on long hikes and I dislike olives and children."

Making the statement on a first date might be too forward and creepy. But waiting for a societally appropriate time, like when marriage is in the cards, will inevitably end in heartbreak and wasted time.

At what point in dating do you tell the other person that you want to die childless?

The only hope for me and my like-minded friends is that somewhere out in the world there is a group of sterile men who just want to adopt puppies and travel the world together until we all die childless and alone.

My Dating Profile

(that doesn't include things like "the outdoors" and "adventures")

Likes:

- The cream top on yogurt.
- Socks without any holes.
- The day after grocery shopping.
- The feeling you get when you think of a word you were trying to remember.
- Perfect snot rockets.
- Putting on flip flops for the first time since last fall.
- Pickles that come extra on a plate of food.
- ChapStick.
- Bananagrams, crosswords, and other puzzles, but only when they're not too hard and only when I win.
- Bicycles, obviously.

Dislikes:

- Finishing a book and feeling like you've lost a best friend.
- Setting something down and immediately forgetting where it is.
- Stepping on a rock inside my sandal.
- Fluorescent lighting.
- Gas station radio.
- When autocorrect is incorrect.
- Wind.
- Flat bicycle tires, obviously.

Breaking the Streak

THE OTHER DAY I was sitting in a coffee shop doing important work on my computer—i.e., staring half-mindlessly out the window—when I decided it was time to ride my bicycle home. I packed up my computer into my bag and slung it over my shoulder and waved goodbye to the friendly neighborhood baristas. I got on my bike for the ten-minute ride to my house and whistled while I pedaled myself home.

As I pushed maybe my fourth downstroke, clouds suddenly gathered and the rain gods decided to let loose. I mean, just let us have it, like someone really pissed them off. Baseball-sized hail started pelting from the sky. Maybe it was a little smaller, but that's what it felt like: baseballs hitting my face.

Cars splashed past me; drivers laughed at my misfortune while I huffed and puffed pathetically onward. I eyeballed anything I could use for shelter, but home was just so close and a warm lonely dog was waiting for me.

My persistence paid off, though, as I finally rolled into my driveway and blasted through my front door, dripping, heaving, baseball-welted, defeated.

I set my wet bag of important electronics on the table, said hi to my pup, turned back around, and I swear to the Storm Gods, the rain had instantly stopped and the gosh darned sun had come out.

This is how my luck has been going as of late.

This bad luck streak semi-started about six months ago with my boyfriend's own misfortune, which he kindly, unintentionally, and apparently gifted to me.

His truck was broken into early one morning and the scumbag thief took a couple thousand dollars' worth of climbing gear—my climbing shoes and back-pack included—a wallet, and a few other items before fleeing to a nearby gas station to fill up his car's tank using my boyfriend's credit card.

But what comes around goes around. Not in the way that karma found Scumbag and he got what was coming for him. No, the guy (or girl) was never caught. When I say "what comes around goes around," I just mean that history repeats itself.

History repeated itself just a few weeks later. It was a Thursday morning—the morning I deliver papers for the newspaper I work for—and it all happened earlyish during an otherwise ordinary day.

I put some water on for coffee, wrangled my dog to use the facilities, and walked outside to greet the morning. When I looked out at my truck, though, I noticed the front driver's side door was resting open. Someone had broken into my truck. Rushing out in my sweatpants and unruly hair, while simultaneously giving a wave and acting cool toward my passing neighbor, I opened the door and saw my center console had been rummaged through. Half its contents were on the driver's seat, including, but not limited to, a half-eaten piece of peanut butter bread, an avocado pit, some ginger candies, a bottle of ibuprofen, a seriously scratched CD, and some possibly used tissues.

In other words, garbage.

Looking through my disheveled truck, I started a mental list in my head of anything that might have been stolen: I'd left my climbing harness, an old camera, some shoes, and a bunch of stuff from a recent camping trip in the back seats. A CD case was somewhere, and maybe some floating dollars? I looked around and saw none of them.

All I saw was the massively tall pile of old newspapers strewn about.

They were old issues I had gathered from my deliveries, and had the thief looked under them, he (or she) would have found that climbing harness, the camera and camping gear, CDs, my climbing helmet, a game of Farkel, and some loose PBRs—all still there.

So then what did the thief take? I really don't think anything... Perhaps a couple crumpled dollar bills?

After my nerves settled, I came to the realization that the thief's luck was worse than mine. Not only had he touched my used Kleenex and old peanut butter bread, but he couldn't seem to stand the idea of looking under the newspaper mountain covering all my high-priced items. I didn't have the heart to tell my boyfriend that what had ultimately caused his bad luck—the cleanliness of his truck—had been the root of my good luck—the not so cleanliness of my own. But regardless, it was a great, albeit messy, end to a terrible streak of luck.

Eating Dirt and Saving Face

LAST WEEK, I endoed on my mountain bike. It was one of those gracefully embarrassing falls where I wasn't doing anything particularly cool. I wasn't impressing anyone. I wasn't trying a new technical move over that sweet jump. It was a slow, stupid, dumb, sloppy tumble.

After my face hit the ground, I came up for air just as gracefully as I went down.

"I'm good, I'm fine!" I yelled to no one, because my friend was nowhere in sight.

When she caught up to me, her look of horror said it all. Though everything was intact, blood was all over my face and smeared on my teeth, which I was baring at her through a nervous smile.

"How does it look?" I asked.

She gagged and suggested we get me home as soon as possible to clean me up.

The next morning, I woke up with swollen, split lips, and I had a constellation of road rash right down the center of my face that only grew more red and much more noticeable as the week went on. The scabs became darker and more apparent, but they hurt less so I also kinda forgot they were there—that is, until I went to get coffee and the barista looked at me and pointed to her own face with raised eyebrows. This, I learned, is the nonverbal equivalent of saying *Oh, shit, what happened to your face?*

Battle wounds are odd. In some weird sadistic way, we want to be proud of them, like *Yeah, I'm a tough cookie for tipping over face first onto the ground because I was doing something cool and badass!* And then everyone is supposed to applaud as you walk by to order your cup of strong black coffee, because that's what badasses drink. And somewhere in my mind, I'm really hoping that people are thinking *Damn, she must have been doing something really rad/gnar/sick/sweetbro to make her face look like that!* even though I know, truly in my heart, that they're actually probably thinking *Ewwww. Gross.*

So, as I take a sip of my strong black coffee and spill it all over the front of my shirt, right in front of every-one, not because it's hot, but because my lips are still an awkwardly larger-than-normal state, I do thank my lucky stars that things aren't worse. I'm thankful that I could ride with my friend back down to the trail-head and laugh about how my bloody lips looked like a beaver, or a walrus. That I can wake up the next morning with only a swollen face, because we've all heard those other horror stories. The broken bones, twisted ankles, bonked heads, and that's the waiver we all sign when we choose to do the things we do.

And we will keep doing them and continue to forget about the law of gravity and physics, and we will keep tipping over, running into trees, and making ourselves bruise and bleed. Then we will get up, wipe ourselves off, and march into that coffee shop, past everyone who is staring, and right up to that bar and order the strongest, blackest cup of coffee we can, with our warrior wounds showing proudly and our bruised egos comfortably hidden deep where no one can see.

Acknowledgments

THESE STORIES were written over many years, and so a couple dozen people contributed to the success of this book. I want to thank every one from the bottom of my heart. If you've been a part of my life, whether I mention you or not, I'm grateful for you.

To Missy and *The Durango Telegraph*. It feels like I was a mere child when Missy took a chance on me, letting me write for Durango's independent weekly. I look back at some of my first stories and am truly surprised that she let them go to print. They're pretty terrible. But, with her edits and her persistent belief in me, I kept writing, learning, and getting better. Thanks to Missy first, for being one of my biggest role models; for staying gritty, grounded, witty, genuine, and keeping her edge. But also for never telling me how bad 1 was when 1 started writing for the paper, and for allowing me to grow into the writer, photographer, and person 1 am today. 1 owe her more than she knows (or maybe she does know).

To Luke, one of my dearest friends, who, over the decade I've known him, has pushed, nagged, and pressured me into writing a book. His own pursuit of writing and publishing has been my beacon, and he steadfastly believed in me and never let me rest until 1 pursued my writing dreams. 1 thank him for all the advice, support, and most importantly, the numerous beers consumed at our regular Carver Brewing happy hours.

To "the compound": Jill, Ted, Kara, and Natan, who have been my support system when 1 needed it most, and contributed to a safe, peaceful oasis through turbulent times. They've kept my head above water, shared food, wine, Manhattans, conversation, laughs, and advice, and allowed me a home in which 1 could safely and peacefully sit down and put this book together.

To my friend Zach, who took a chance on me by publishing this book. 1 put him through a lot during this process, and 1 learned a lot, too: that 1 don't know as much about punctuation as 1 thought 1 did, and to always try to stay flexible, open-minded, and humble. Thank you for convincing me that my stories might resonate with others, make some folks laugh, or just look good as a book sitting on top of a coffee table. I can't wait to put this book on my coffee table.

I can't wait to own a coffee table.

And to all my fellow bicycle nerds in Durango. Thank you for always being there to answer my many weird questions and to help me buy new bikes, sell old ones, and continue to fix my current ones. Thank you for riding with me, taking me on scary trails, allowing me to crash, and not judging me too much when I cry on my bicycle. You all are gems.

JENNAYE DERGE is a writer, photographer, and very average bicycle rider. She enjoys making mundane things a little more colorful through dirty words, stupid jokes, and, every so often, intelligent witticisms. She's learned over the years that there is a time and a place for these things. Sometimes she cares. Oftentimes she doesn't.

Jennaye grew up in Colorado and prefers living her life as such. She loves getting after it outside on her mountain bike, skiing groomers (and the occasional powder or backcountry day), and running and climbing if she has the rare itch. She also enjoys hiding indoors, reading a book, daydreaming, and drinking coffee or tea with her dog, Calvin, snuggled next to her.

She is a passionate bicycle commuter and currently the publisher of *Ride Your Bike! Zine* and developer of Bike Durango, an organization helping people ride bicycles more and drive cars less.

You can learn about her and her projects at jennayederge.com and on Instagram @jennaye_d.

CASA URRACA PRESS publishes creative nonfiction, poetry, photography, and other works by authors we believe in. New Mexico and the US Southwest are rich in creative and literary talent, and the rest of the world deserves to experience our perspectives. So we champion books that belong in the conversation— books with the power, compassion, and variety to bring very different people closer together.

We are proudly centered in the high desert somewhere near Abiquiu, New Mexico. Visit us at casaurracapress.com for exquisite editions of our books and to register for workshops with our authors.

CPSIA information can be obtained
at www.ICGtesting.com
Printed in the USA
LVHW030424310522
720041LV00004B/685

9 781956 375060